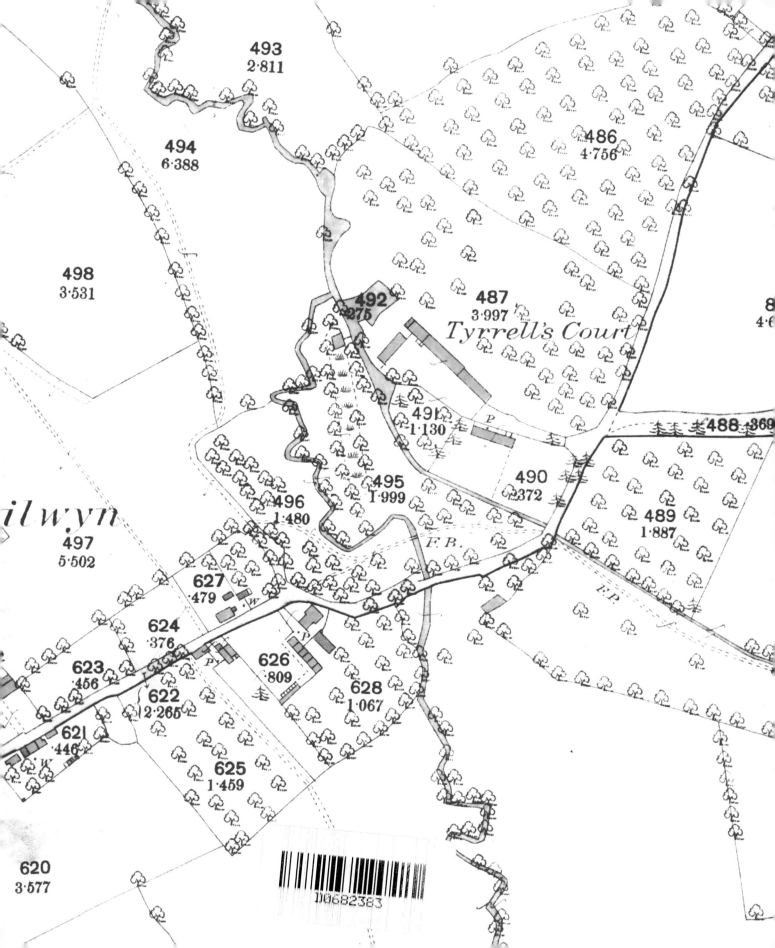

ONE POTATO, TWO...

Finding the Magic

by William Chase

First published in Great Britain in 2015 by
Single Estate Publishing Ltd
Rosemaund Farm, Preston Wynne, Herefordshire, HR1 3PG
www.williamschase.co.uk

ISBN 978-0-9934301-0-7

Designed, printed and bound in Great Britain by Orphans Press Ltd

Orphans Press supports the Forest Stewardship Council® (FSC®), the
leading international forest-certification organisation. Our books carrying
the FSC label are printed on FSC® - certified paper.

To my parents, Sam and Leonard Chase.

Contents

Finding the magic

A few years ago, when I first toyed around with the idea of writing a book, I was told to find my focus. Should I try and empower budding entrepreneurs? I've spoken to so many people who all tend to ask me the same questions. Where do I get my ideas? How did I finance my business and market my products, and what made me want to work for myself in the first place?

Or perhaps a memoir would be a better fit for me – one where I tell my story of misspent youth, my years of bad business decisions that ended in bankruptcy to founding Tyrrells Chips and Williams Chase Distillery?

Others thought that a book of cocktail recipes was a better option, or maybe a lifestyle tome celebrating Herefordshire in all its green-grassed beauty?

While all of these ideas had merit, none felt like the right fit for the story I wanted to tell. My life has been so varied that I didn't feel I could be pigeonholed into any of them. Since I've never been one to follow the rules, I decided to put all of the above and more into one book as it's all about finding the magic and DNA. A good brand is like a person with charisma, the more you get to know it the better it gets.

There is, however, a common thread: potatoes. They're not pretty. They're a pain to plant, harvest and sell. But I wouldn't be where I am today without them – from farming and trading spuds in my younger days to making potato chips and more recently distilling vodka and gin at the first distillery of its kind in the UK.

Like all stories of this nature, the road has been bumpy, with many highs and lows along the way. One Potato, Two... is a celebration of entrepreneurship, Herefordshire and family. And, of course, the humble spud.

William Chase, October 2015

THE GOOD LIFE

Growing up in Herefordshire

Me and my sister Caroline and our dog Suzy
in 1966 at Tyrrell's Court.

" Where's the brute? "

I grew up at Tyrrell's Court, our family farm near Dilwyn in Herefordshire, England. In many ways it was an idyllic start to life. My mother, Sheila Jean (who was affectionately known as Sam), and father, Leonard Thomas, had bought the farm ten years before I was born, though it owned us just as much as we owned it.

While Sam and Leonard worked the farm (cattle, turkeys, and chickens) and crops (flowers in poly tunnels, perry pears, cider apples, potatoes, cereals and Brussel sprouts), I spent my days buildings dams in the brook that ran through the property, making up my own games in the many different buildings or tormenting my two older sisters, Caroline and Fiona. From an early age, I also needed to lend a hand, whether it be helping my mum make jam, freezing fresh veg or feeding the animals, we all pitched in to do whatever was needed.

Everything at Tyrrell's Court was dictated by the seasons. Spring was fragrant with the smell of freshly turned soil as the farmers did their planting. On the dinner table we'd find lamb chops, runner beans, and new potatoes, all drowning in a delicious rich gravy. Freshly picked rhubarb was stewed and served as a crumble for dessert, everything cooked in the Aga. Summer was heady with freshly picked strawberries, cut grass, pungent potato heads and meadow hay. Gooseberry fool, all homemade, was served with vanilla ice cream.

Autumn was synonymous with the cider apple and perry pear harvest - the fruit would begin to ferment as soon as it was picked. Open fires kept us warm in winter and hearty stews kept us full. Our pantry was stocked year round and everything we needed for the cooler months was dried, preserved or frozen in a big box freezer. Our chickens provided us with eggs regardless of the season. If we ever had any leftover baked potatoes, my mum would fry them up the next day with eggs for breakfast.

In spite of all this, however, I was fairly difficult as a child. I never liked being told what to do and I felt very territorial of my home and our land. Always happier in my own company or doing things I wanted to do, When the Guest sisters from next door would enquire 'Where's the brute?' when they popped over for a cup of tea and a natter and I was nowhere to be seen.

School wasn't the right thing for me either. I was not a talented student and being locked indoors didn't suit me at all. I spent my days longing to be back at the farm or daydreaming about getting older and being free and in control of my own destiny. When I was twelve, I started my first business. With my mother's help, I bought a mix of 100 Aylesbury and Khaki Campbell duck chicks. Each day I'd feed them with mashed potato and water to stuff them up. When they were ready, I'd take them to market. Mr Peachy in Ludlow and Benjamin Bunny in Hereford were my two major customers. The latter of which would slaughter and butcher them in the cellars below the market. I replaced whatever I sold with new chicks and the cycle continued.

When I was a little bit older, I started tinkering with decrepit vintage tractors. No longer any use to their previous owners (the farmers had all moved on to newer shinier models), I'd find them rust-ridden and abandoned in fields and hedges all over the countryside. Too young to drive, I enlisted my dad's help to ship them back to the farm, where I had no ulterior motive other than to bring these old beasts back to life. I'd start by taking the engine apart and cleaning all the parts before reassembling the lot. If that didn't work, I'd enlist the help of other knowledgeable farmers, pore over logbooks and manuals, and do my best to sort out the problem. I always managed to get the tractors back on their tyres, even if it was just for a few smoke-filled seconds before their engines died and another challenge presented itself.

My world, came to a crashing halt when, at the age of 16, my mother passed away from cancer. Sheila had been the person I could truly relate to in my younger years and her loss was a massive blow. Despite my father's coaxing, I never went back to school following her death. Instead, I went to work for a local farmer. In the Autumn, I harvested apples and in the winter I was a skivvy for his beef farm – for which I was paid £21.50 a week. It was backbreaking and thankless work, but it did teach me three very important life lessons: the first was that I never wanted to work for anybody else; the second was that I wanted to continue farming; and the third was that I needed to get some kind of qualifications if I was to be taken seriously.

At 18, I enrolled in a basic agriculture course, where I was taught things like animal husbandry and crop health. I thought I was wasting my time in classes during the week, while rushing back to Herefordshire on the weekend to earn money, which mostly consisted of chopping up firewood and other odd jobs. Though looking back I did, however, learn how other people did things and gave myself a small amount of space to grow up – even if my first time getting out into the big wide world was only to be in the county next door.

A year later I was ready to begin my first solo venture. My mum had left me a small parcel of land, no more than thirty acres, but that wasn't enough for my big ideas. Instead, I borrowed some money, leased a tractor and rented my services to local farmers. There were many downsides to this type of work that were not limited to the 18-hour days, immense loneliness and the feeling that I was never going to get ahead. On the upside, I was able to build my network and get a better understanding of the local environment, which proved invaluable for the future.

My mother, Sam.

My father, Leonard Chase, bought this tractor new in 1960, the year I was born

I also luckily had access to some of the older farmers who loved nothing more than having a natter. They'd come out to the field, armed with a batch of cakes, and give me their take on the world. I'd been struggling to make ends meet and speaking with them gave me a lot of solace. On one hot summer's day, with the smell of the engine oil mingling with the freshly cut grass, I got a lot of comfort from talking to one particular farmer. As I took a break and we both leaned up against a tractor wheel, he confessed to waking up at 4am in a panic over the amount of money he owed. It was a great relief for me to hear this because I'd been having the same problem and I thought I was the only one.

It was also through these guys that I learnt what hard work was. Michael Mercer, a local progressive farmer who I used to contract for, once stopped me as I was going home one day on my tractor at 7pm. '12 hours a day isn't enough,' he said. 'You should be working 18 if you want to get ahead.' I was already knackered and knew I needed to do something different. Potatoes seemed like the answer to me, despite the warnings. 'Spuds were a wishing crop,' they would say. 'You either wished you had more, because they were attracting such a high price, or you wished you had less, because you had too many to get rid of.' Another popular saying was that potatoes were; either a pop and cockles or a champagne and oysters crop. I liked the sound of the latter - and since I was looking for a cash crop with a high yield - this was to be my next move.

As soon as I had a plan, I took this advice with me - along with my network and rudimentary bookkeeping skills (a paper and carbon ledger was all I used at the time) and I threw myself into potato farming. It's only when you look back that you can see life's turning points – and this is a big one for me. To be honest, I didn't have any great love for spuds one way or the other, but I hoped growing them might be more profitable and less time consuming and labour intensive than what I'd been doing. As far as I could tell, the yield you get with potatoes, when linked with demand, had huge potential to make money.

I began renting fields off farmers that I knew. The latter was a pioneering move at the time. It wasn't seen as proper to let another farmer rent your land, but it helped that I was a known entity. Because of my relationships, I knew what land was available, and because I was respected for the work I'd already done, they didn't mind giving me a chance.

By the time I was 20, I'd had a chat with my dad about Tyrrell's Court. He was interested in selling, and I was interested in taking it over, but angry that he wouldn't give it to me. It was, after all, the place that I had grown up on and the land had belonged to my family since before I was born. I couldn't imagine it not being a part of us going forward, so instead of letting a stranger come in and take it from us, I secured a loan from a bank manager for £200,000 and begrudgingly bought it from him instead – though he did give me a discount.

Looking back, it was the right decision for him to make. I was only 20 and had to take on a massive loan. I had no experience, though did have my own ideas and thought if I worked hard, I'd make money. Unfortunately, all of my cash was tied up in a 100 per cent mortgage. I had nothing to trade with so I spent years weaving and bobbing, constantly reaching the limits as soon as any money came in. These days, I'm not sure if many banks would trust a sole trader with no experience with a 100 per cent mortgage, but they were willing to take a chance back then.

Life took on a natural progression after that. The years began to mesh together as the seasons passed. Planting, harvesting and selling. In many ways, it was how life was supposed to be. I met my first wife, Sarah, and we had two sons. Harry was born in 1986 and James came along in 1990. Along with the joy of having a family, I was also very aware of my new responsibilities as a husband and father. We were just about getting by on the farm, but I dreamt of expansion: more fields meant more potatoes.

After a few years and with some financial help, my business eventually grew big enough to start thinking about building a cold storage unit. This was the golden ticket that would allow us to supply supermarkets all year round. I was on the cusp of having it installed when my financial backing fell out from beneath me and I nearly lost everything.

In 1992, the Queen famously announced that the year had been an *annus horribilus*, and it was pretty much the same for us as well. It rained all day every day, which meant that I couldn't get my spuds out of the ground and had no product to sell. Our funds were at an all time low and I'd been ducking and diving, trying to escape creditors and cutting costs were I could. I'd borrowed a lot of money trying to keep afloat and was doing a lot of the manual labour myself.

It was then that I had my accident. I fell off the grading machine, which gave me a bad back that I later exacerbated by lifting some farming equipment. The result? I ended up paralysed in hospital – I couldn't feel anything from the waist down. I spent four weeks bedridden thankful that my legs were healing but also aware that I was about to be declared bankrupt. I knew it was coming and there was nothing that I could do about it. I was crushed.

An official receiver was appointed to come and take everything I owned. Somehow I managed to keep my car, which I sold for £10,000. I used it to buy groceries, a £250 Subaru pickup with rust holes in the floor and then I ran away to Australia.

I was in so much debt that I couldn't see a way out. I was tortured by suicidal thoughts while searching for something that could provide me with a solution for my massive problems. It was then that I read an ad in the Farmers' Weekly. An English expat was looking for help in Australia, so I headed for Geraldton – an isolated town in the middle of nowhere on the country's west coast. It was only my second time outside of the UK. When I picked my car up in Perth, the guy behind the desk told me to 'watch out for the 'roos, mate. They'll bounce off your bonnet, knock your engine out and you'll die out there.' I spent the five-hour drive petrified and things didn't get much better when I reached my destination.

The land was desolate and dry, and the farmer was an old-generation Yorkshireman who'd lived Down Under for thirty years, though he was yet to lose the lilt to his accent. I'd never been anywhere so isolated. Inside the house was a pastiche of everything English, while outside his land ran to the horizon and the only change in the scenery were the trains that ran through his property twice a day. I lasted 48 hours.

When I left the UK, my wife wasn't sure I was going to be coming back and she wasn't interested in coming with me. In my mind, I was doing a reccie, planning for a new life for all of us. But instead of returning to England after my failed meeting in Geralton, I booked a ticket to Brisbane to see an old friend who'd emigrated a few years before and was working just outside of the city.

While I was there, I spent a lot of time looking about for new opportunities. I met another farmer, a guy in his 70s who was farming 1000 acres of cotton. He was on a big roll and wanted somebody to take it on. It was really tempting as all I wanted was a new life and never to see another potato again. It was the pull of my two little boys, Harry and James, however, that got me back on the plane and to face my responsibilities. Four weeks after running away, I returned to the UK.

Where do you start when you have nothing? I had no choice but to get back to work. I still had a few farmers that I did work for, so they paid me a little bit, and there was still about £5,000 left over from the sale of my car. It was then that I began to trade potatoes – buying them from the farmers and then selling them on to supermarkets and other third parties. It wasn't ideal, but it was the only skill I had and potatoes were all I really knew about.

What I really wanted, however, was to hold onto Tyrrell's Court. The land was already lost, but I didn't want to lose the house and buildings as this was my home and I was going to fight for it. Herefordshire, being the small close-knit community that it is, everybody knows everybody else's business and the vultures were gathering – even some of the people who I thought I could trust turned out not to be on my side. While the bank was trying to sell the property through a local agent, I would do my best to make Tyrrell's Court look as unappealing and as unprofitable as possible.

When I knew people were coming to look at the place, I'd knock slates off the roof and let the lawn grow to make it look as dilapidated as possible and discourage potential buyers. Luckily I hadn't signed a tenancy form with the bank, so I had a few months to get the money together. This was quite a difficult task given my reputation, but I didn't want someone

Planting potatoes in Herefordshire's red soil, 2002

buying it from underneath me. It was a different story when I had people coming out to see if they would give me a loan. I'd make the whole place look idyllic - replacing the roof tiles and sprucing everything up to look its best.

It's true that when you're at your lowest and most needy point, you find out who will stick by and support you. After my mother died, my father remarried. I was never that nice to my stepmother to start with, but it was she and a friend of hers who stepped in and guaranteed my loan with Barclay's. It's all about relationships and the ability to find and sell the magic - even when talking to a bank manager.

This was also the case with the farmers I worked with. When I knew bankruptcy was inevitable, I thought of ten farmers who I thought would stick with me through the crisis - and only three did. The rest treated me as though I was a leper, which was hurtful, but understandable.

To get back on my feet was an amazing character building exercise. The farmers who came to my rescue supported me by renting me land or selling me their

potatoes if they thought I could help them find better markets. It sounds a bit clichéd, but these people restored my faith in humanity and showed me that to succeed we need confidence and belief in ourselves.

Pat Lees is worth a particular mention. When it comes to trading potatoes, she was my saviour. Pat owned a small business called Herbert Twycross that used to pack potatoes for Tesco. It was a simple business, but a very effective one. Pat agreed to buy my spuds and to pay me within a week, which made it possible to buy stock from other farmers to trade.

I was in the right place at the right time for Pat too. Herefordshire was producing beautiful potatoes while England's traditional growing areas had been infected with a fungal disease and large retailers were looking elsewhere for their product. We also sold our potatoes clean-skinned, which suited the supermarkets. This was around the same time that the public stopped shopping locally at small grocery stores and went to the likes of Tesco and Sainsbury's instead. At the supermarkets all the produce had to look perfect as soon as their customers stepped through their air-conditioned doors as shoppers were now buying veg on aesthetics not taste.

So, safe with a big loan and the help of a great bank manager in Hereford, I got Tyrrell's Court back as a limited company and was allowed to rent storage, though they didn't want me to grow or trade potatoes, as the bank thought this was too risky. Instead I set up another small business on the side, starting with 10 acres that grew to 500 over the next 10 years. By the end, I had my own fleet of lorries and three mobile phones the size of house bricks that were constantly ringing. I was making decent money, though I didn't enjoy it. I had to put up with farmers complaining that their loads were being rejected, while on the other side the supermarkets tried to squeeze me on price.

The very nature of the business meant that everyday I was starting from scratch, and even though I was making enough money to service my debt on the loan and live fairly well for Herefordshire, I felt morally - for want of a better term - bankrupt. It was great that I could afford to send my boys to a good school, but I wasn't building or creating anything. Something

had to change, which was a strange new situation for me to find myself in. When I first started the business, I would've given anything to own my house and have a stable income, but it wasn't enough any more.

My eureka moment came when I had a load of potatoes rejected from McCain's. The spuds fried 'too dark' for their exacting standards. I had a distressed farmer on my hands and what I thought was thousands of worthless spuds. In the end, I sold them to Kettle Chips. They were making hand-fried chips and they were buying potatoes at a great margin. I ended up selling them 30 lorry loads and couldn't help but think that this was an amazing business. Naturally, I thought 'why can't I do that?.' I quickly realised there was no reason I couldn't, so I did - with the help of the same bank manager who was happy to support me as by then I had paid off some of the debt and I needed £800k to build my factory.

STARTING TYRRELL'S

My first eureka moment

My first eureka moment

It was October 2001 when I first had the idea to start a chip factory and Tyrrell's was up and running six months later in April 2002. I surprised myself by how fast I managed to turn a shed full of potatoes into a working factory with a brand. I didn't stop until it was all up and running. This was my shot, and I was going to take it.

People often ask me if I was scared of taking such a big risk. Strangely, I wasn't. Of course there are always niggles of self-doubt and nervousness when you embark on something new. The difference this time was that I was a lot more experienced. I was excited by the prospect of entering a new field with my potatoes at the very core of it. The only second thoughts I remember having were after our first production run. I'd asked all the guys on the farm to help and by the end of the day we had made our first batch and I wondered if anyone was going to buy it and why they would want to.

By the time I struck on my eureka idea for Tyrrell's, it had been ten years since starting again from scratch, and since then I'd had a reasonable amount of success trading potatoes. Unfortunately, even though I was good at trading and the banks were talking to me again, it was not a business that I felt passionate

about and I didn't like the person it was turning me into.

Potato trading, like any commodity business, is tough: you're only as good as the product you're selling; you have to know your market inside and out; and you have to foster good relationships with all stakeholders. Being a middleman is always a challenge and the daily cut and thrust of the business stretched my moral and ethical boundaries far more than I liked. It's impossible to make everybody happy on these types of exchanges – someone always gets screwed and I had to make sure it wasn't me while maintaining stressful relationships between me, the farmers I represented and the supermarkets I sold to. Not an enviable task, to say the least.

Potato trading did, however, give me a solid understanding of how business works and it prepared me well for what was to follow. I learnt that for any business to succeed there had to be both demand and margin. For me, that meant creating desire with a product that I could be proud of while also making enough money to not only keep my business going, but to make a profit. On top of learning how to turn 50p into a pound, I also came to the realisation that one-off deals were no good to anybody. Good relationships are the only thing that ensures long-term success and repeat business is the cornerstone of this. It's not until I have worked with a particular customer three times that I think that we've built the basis for an enduring relationship.

So, when the idea to start a premium chips company came about, I felt ready. I had a gut feeling that it would work and was willing once again to throw everything at it to make it a success. Yes, there were naysayers, including some of the people who were closest to me at the time, but I couldn't be swayed. I needed to escape and this was my way out. My aim was to make something genuine, tangible and of substance. Nothing riles me more than brands that claim that they're something they're not – and so many of them do it, relying on the marketing's smoke and mirrors and the fact that very few people bother to look any deeper than what they're told. My upbringing had taught me the benefits of eating real food and that's what I wanted to create with Tyrrell's.

And I'd done the maths. If Tyrrell's sold £1m per year, I'd make 20 per cent profit. Not only would I be £200,000 richer per year, which was considerably more than what I'd been making trading potatoes, I'd also be creating something that was sustainable, could be built upon and, most importantly, that I believed in.

But where should I start? While I knew the ins and outs of the potato industry, I had no idea how to go about setting up a food production factory or how to fry chips, both of which I had to sort out before I gave a thought to packaging, distribution and marketing the end product.

Early on in my research, I learnt that a couple of small chip factories were up for sale and I jumped at the chance to make one of them my own. There was one that was, and is still, located in Devon. As chance would have it, I'd recently bought

Grading potatoes, 2001

Planting potatoes at Tyrrell's, 2003

a flat by the sea in Salcombe, Devon, which was not far from the factory. In my mind's eye, I could see my self moving there and starting afresh – it was a heady proposition that spurred me into action. I quickly secured a loan from the bank and put my plans into action. The sale, however, didn't go my way and I reconsidered my options. I'd do it on my own. It was time to look further afield.

These days you could go online and get most of the answers you'd need to start up almost anything. Back then Google was in its naissance and as such wasn't much help to me. The only way I was going to get any kind of foothold was to visit the library or sneak into a factory after dark, neither of which I had much inclination for.

Instead, I followed my nose to the US. I'd heard that there was a number of manufacturers Stateside who might be useful, so within a week of having the idea, I hopped on a plane. First stop: Massachusetts. Cape Cod, if you've never been there, it is instantly recognisable, having been featured in so many films, including *Jaws*. The Cape Cod Potato Chips factory was my draw card. Not only did they make the kind of chips I was interested in producing, they offered factory tours to tourists. Unfortunately, their good will did not extend to helping out an overseas visitor trying to start his own operation and when I began asking probing questions about fryers, potato graders and packaging equipment, they politely sent me on my way (though I did get a souvenir mug out of the deal).

Down, but not out, I headed to New York where I thought I could do a bit more research before making my way home. And Good's Potato Chips is what I found during my stay. I called them up immediately and received a much more welcoming reception. The next day I was on a train to Philadelphia.

Jerry, Dennis, Ian, Hudson and me setting up
the factory in Spring 2002

The path eventually led me to meet Hudson Smith – who is the closest thing I've ever met to being a real cowboy. Wrinkly of face, and leather-booted, he lived in the hill country around Philly and knew of two chip manufacturers that would be more than happy to show me the ropes. He took me to see Hers and Goods in New Holland. He told me that both businesses had been in operation for over 100 years and that they fried their chips in beef dripping. Nothing, however, could have prepared me for the sight I was about to witness.

The factories were kitted out with all the machinery that I'd expected, the only thing that surprised me were the employees. Hers and Goods employed Amish women, who came to work each day in long dark dresses and pinafores, with bonnets on their heads and clogs on their feet. It was quite something to behold. I met the owners who were extremely proud to have just developed their first flavoured potato chip – it was barbecue, naturally. I felt like I'd stepped back in time as I was guided through the process and all my questions were answered, including where I could source my equipment.

Newly informed, my next port of call was Pine Bluffs in Colorado – a tiny town not far from Denver that boasts year-round big blue skies and staggering views of The Rockies looming in the distance. This was Middle America.

The company that made the equipment was a small family-run enterprise operated by many brothers. Our first meeting was at a local diner, where I sat surrounded by each and every one of them and they asked me incredulous questions such as if it was true that in England we drive on the wrong side of the road.

Cultural oddities aside, I could tell that they were the real deal when they showed me around their workshop. The brothers didn't employ any other labour, probably because there were so many of them, and they made everything by hand. Although they mainly produced various agricultural machinery, I'd finally found what I'd been looking for. In addition to making the line for me, they offered to come to the UK and show me how to use it once it was installed. The whole thing would cost £500,000 of the £1m I'd raised through my potato trading profits and a bank loan for the project. I hired them on the spot.

It wasn't until later that I discovered they'd also made the factory line for a few of my early competitors in the UK. Not that it would've changed my mind. I ordered everything I needed from them and hot-footed it back to Blighty to work on the next stage of the business.

Once the kit was ordered it felt as though it was all coming together. It was time to pick a name. After much deliberation, I decided to call the brand Tyrrell's after Tyrrell's Court, the farm I'd been brought up on and bought from my father when I was 19 – and it was also to become the site of the factory once the equipment arrived.

The decision to call the brand Tyrrell's was a big one. I'd spoken to a few brand designers, who took their ideas from other chips and crisp producers and cobbled together their own, not very original, ideas. I didn't take to any of them and decided to go my own way instead. I liked the alliteration of Chase Chips, but Tyrrell's was where I landed. As soon as I had the brand, I had a sign made and put it at the end of my drive.

By this time, I'd all but moved on from my potato trading business. I'd left our best clients with a colleague and threw myself in with everything I had to making Tyrrell's more than just a good idea. It was November 2001, and I'd already jumped one major hurdle. The next was to find some customers.

Tyrrell's first batch, 2001

I'm sure you've heard that old adage: you've got to fake it until you make it. And that's exactly what I did. I was a bit ambitious with respect to timings after I got back from the States – I'd booked myself in to appear at a food show in four months time. As the date rolled around, it soon became clear that I wasn't going to have a product to show. So, instead of pulling out at the last minute, I mocked up packets so we had something to photograph for our promotional material. I also bought a

fish and chip fryer so that I could make samples. There wasn't much more I could do, apart from sell my story, until the equipment arrived and it was paramount that we were up and running as a brand first.

In April 2002, we began making our chips. At the beginning I didn't hire anybody I didn't know, so there was no one on board with a food production background. There were just five employees who I'd selected off the farm and we did everything

from scratch, learning and making mistakes as we went.

After the kit arrived, our gas supply turned out to be our first big challenge. Our beautiful, handmade fryers were built to run on natural gas, but because we we're in the sticks all we had on offer was propane, which burns a lot hotter than its cooler cousin. It also explodes when it burns. We nearly set fire to the whole lot a couple of times before we figured out the problem – and it turned out to be a great mistake to have as once we'd mastered the machinery, the chips turned out to be fantastic.

And then there was the art of achieving a curl. This was high on the American's list of must-haves for the perfect potato chip. It was in nobody's interest, after all, that we produce a flat, greasy crisp. The secret here is batch cooking. Once the potatoes are sliced and ready to go, they're loaded into the fryer, which causes the temperature to drop. The chips begin to curl as the potato slices heat up again. We learnt very quickly when it was the exact right time to remove them from the fryer. I'd tell you more, but I don't want to give all of the secrets away.

Our next big issue was packaging. I didn't have any preconceived ideas of how a chip packet should look. I went into supermarkets to see what other people were doing, but ended up with my own ideas for the pack. At first I wanted to turn the whole market on its head by packaging the crisps in printed cardboard cubes (see below). In theory, this idea was sound – nobody else was doing it and I thought it would be a great way to stand out. In practice, however, the cubes didn't display well and cost us a lot in waste packaging, so we scrapped that idea and went with our first transparent packs instead.

I knew back then, and I still believe it now, that if you've got a good story to share, you should tell it. From day one, our story was printed on the back of our packets, including my email address so customers could write to me with their thoughts – a surprising number of which did.

Getting the chips into the packets, however, proved quite the challenge. We didn't have the right machinery – or didn't know how to use the one we had properly – and about one in every five packets was a complete failure, with chips caught in the bottom or top of the packets (at best) or a batch of freshly fried chips ending up on the floor (at worst). It doesn't sound like much as I write this now, but at the time, when all you want is for things to work, it's the little irks such as these that can really get you down.

The teething problems quickly sorted themselves out, which allowed us to move onto more enjoyable quests, such as coming up with our flavours. For our first foray into the chip producing world, we started with four: lightly salted, chilli, cheese, and seasalt and cider vinegar. It's a common belief among chip and crisp manufacturers that anything featuring cheese is going to be your biggest seller, but once again we bucked the trend.

For the first two years, our seasalt and cider vinegar chips outsold the rest and basically kept the business afloat. We could never get the cheese flavour as perfect as we wanted it to be, but the vinegar chips filled the air with the smell of the seaside, as if you'd just unwrapped a newspaper bundle of piping hot fish and chips. Thankfully the whole country agreed – people went mad for them.

Tyrrell's new packaging, 2005

Me and Ian Parkinson, holding our first award

Before I go any further I should probably talk about the difference between chips and crisps. Many understandably think that it's an American English versus British English thing, but they'd be wrong. Crisps and chips are two different snacks and what we were making were chips by definition.

Yes, chips do come from America. Although their origins are a little murky, it's a commonly held belief that restaurateur and chef George Crum invented the potato chip in the mid-1800s in Saratoga Springs, New York. According to the most popular story, a customer at Crum's restaurant kept asking for his fried potato slices to be thinner and thinner, which Crum did, whittling them down as far as he could by hand before throwing them in the fryer. Afraid that his customer wasn't going to like his new creation in spite of his strange request, he loaded them up with salt before serving. He needn't have worried - his potato chips were a resounding success and a new snack was born.

So, when potatoes are hand cut and fried, they're chips. Crisps are made in a similar fashion, but with one extra step. Once the potatoes are sliced, they're then washed in a saline tank to remove all the starch. This is so when they're fried they always come out white. Unfortunately, this removes a lot of the flavour and means that the crisp soaks up more oil as soon as it's removed from the fryer. This means that crisps have about 40 per cent of fat compared to 14 per cent in hand-fried chips.

Once we were up and running and making money, the fun really started. It's in my nature to experiment. I've never been happy resting on my laurels. Not long after we perfected our chips, Mario, one of my staff members found a couple of parsnips in the bottom of a load of potatoes, so he sliced them up and fried them. They were so good that we tried out other vegetables as well and our root chips entered the market and were an instant hit. This was a huge boon for our business because they sold for twice the price of the potato chips and helped the company double its margin. It also helped that people thought they were the healthier option too - a fact that we like to poke fun at on our packets, you can eat these as part of your five-a-day, we'd say, as long as you get off the couch, exercise and eat your broccoli.

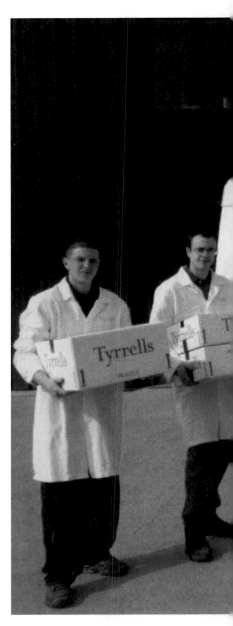

The first year Tyrrell's team, 2002. Dick Jones and Rachel Davies not pictured

The Tyrrell's team, 2005

I've always hated corporate speak and much prefer to have some fun with my brands and the people who purchase my products.

We always had fun with our packaging. Our naked chips were the first to get a makeover. I found a Victorian picture of naked ladies that worked really well. When that proved a success we went on the hunt for other eccentric photos to put on our chips. My son Harry found the picture of three northern ladies selling cheese at a farmers' market, which was a favourite of mine. We did have some complaints that some of them were too risqué, but that only led to more press and the overwhelming majority of the people who bought our chips saw the fun in it.

In fact, building personal relationships was the backbone of our business. In terms of finding customers to stock our chips in the beginning, timing and luck played a critical part in the success of Tyrrell's. The economy was on the rise again and the countryside was booming as a result. It was the start of the 'shop local' movement and farm shops and delicatessens were popping up all over the country and I had a feeling these were the types of people who would want to work with us.

We couldn't afford distributors as they sucked too much money out of our margins, so we did all the legwork ourselves. As I said before, Google was no help. The Yellow Pages was where I started. There's an art to finding the perfect customer and I soon learnt who were the right ones to target. All the people who bought from me in the very beginning were looking for something genuine with pedigree. They didn't want what the supermarkets stocked and they wanted the personal touch. It also helped that my product was 100 per cent British made – and delicious.

I remember on one road trip around Sussex walking into a very smart looking deli where the owner was serving. I didn't realise until the person in front of me started talking that he was a sales rep. I'm not sure what he was selling, but as soon as he had her attention he went into his corporate spiel and the owner told him quickly to leave her alone in no uncertain terms. So, when it was my turn to speak with her, I made it brief. I introduced myself, gave her a sample box, asked her to have a taste and if she thought they were any good she could give me a call, which she later did. As a result of this single experience, I learnt that the best way of dealing with independents was to talk to them as friends.

We spent all our time driving to meet our customers and selling our chips. It was a fantastic time to be launching a business because the feel-good factor in the country was brilliant. I must also hasten to add here that our likability wasn't the only reason they were keen to work with us. Not only was there very little competition at the time, we also offered a 100 per cent profit: we would sell them a bag of our chips for £1 and they'd retail them for £2. It was a rare case of win-win. Avoiding distributors also meant that the shops got their chips quicker. It wasn't unusual for the potatoes to be dug in the morning, in the fryer at lunchtime and in the shop by the afternoon. We didn't have to store anything. Everything was with the customer within 48 hours.

We loved our independent retailers and they loved us right back. Legges of Bromyard, a fine food emporium and butcher also in Herefordshire, put a display of our chips in the middle of their front door so that their customers had to literally skirt around it to get into the shop. Loyalty was also strong among our customers, and they expected it from us too. One day we got a phone call that turned out to be a kind of ransom demand. A deli in a small town, was disgruntled that we'd started supplying their competitor located just across the road. So, the next time Rolf, our aged delivery driver, came in with their order, they locked him in a cupboard and wouldn't let him out until we agreed that they would be our only customer. It was all tongue in cheek – right down to the muffled sounds of Rolf banging on the door – but we agreed on the spot. Small businesses, directs as we called them, were the backbone of our business and had to be supported.

Not that it stopped the big boys from trying to get us on their shelves. It was in 2006 that I learnt that Tesco was stocking our products. This was back when the big discount supermarkets were less ethical than they are now. These days a lot of people care where their food has come from – buying local is particularly important. A small, but vocal minority also want to know that the farmers and other producers were not being taken advantage of. This has changed the way the big chains operate, but at the time it was very different.

I didn't want to deal with the big discounters because I felt that they would undermine my product and also affect sales at the farm shops and other purveyors of fine food that had supported us from the beginning. I was happy to deal with Waitrose because they sold Tyrrell's at full price, but was not interested in dealing with any of the other big hitters. We were selling well and had little competition, so there was no need to expand further than that.

The people at Tesco, however, had other ideas. I'm not sure how they managed it, but the company bought a couple of lorry loads of our chips on the grey market. They had asked us previously if we would consider supplying to them, but our answer was always a resounding no. When I complained they invited me into their offices for a chat.

Mark Hammond irrigating
Herefordshire potatoes, 2002

I've said it before, but I think it's worth stating again. Building relationships with the people I deal with is very important to me. And, while it would by ungentlemanly to divulge too much of what happened in that meeting, I will say that I was not impressed with the way I was treated. On a business level, however, they advised me that they were going to continue to stock our chips, but that I had to get my prices down – and if we did that they'd be able to give us ta few millions pounds worth of business. It was a tough decision to make, but in the end I told them no. It wasn't worth all the hard work I'd put in to building a successful business, but I was nervous about going up against such a mammoth organisation.

As far as I know only two companies have ever been asked to be delisted from Tesco – Levi's Jeans and Tyrrell's. It was after talking to my PR agency that I realised that there might be a story in this. I was mostly annoyed that Tesco, who were making so much money at the time, were trying to undercut my business and I was sure that was how they were dealing with everyone else too. My general feeling was that Sir Terry Leahy (the former Tesco CEO) got his knighthood by keeping the price of food down, which meant screwing over the farmers.

One of the national broadsheets was the first newspaper to print the story – in a tiny little box in the weekend edition. To be honest, this was a disappointment. When I first spoke to them about the story, they'd led me to believe it would be a full-page feature. I didn't want to think about the money I'd spent with the agency just to get the story out there with so little return.

And then, on Sunday night, the phone started ringing. I have no idea how they got my number, but that evening I took at least ten calls from newspapers and TV and radio programmes. The following morning I was on BBC Radio 4's Today show along with the Bishop of Canterbury. I spoke to many other radio and TV stations too and I was trending on the BBC website all day. In all, I did 27 interviews. Everyone was interested in the farmer who snubbed Tesco, but there was also some luck involved. I doubt the story would've garnered much attention if something terrible had happened at the same time. Tesco did eventually apologise and agreed to not sell Tyrrell's chips anymore. And they stuck to their agreement until after I sold the company. After that we concentrated on building our brand and adding new products, such as Tyrrell's Alternatives. These included things like dips, nuts and peas. It was a fantastic way of extending our brand in all our independent retailers.

"Victory for independent crisp maker over Tesco

An upmarket crisp maker today claimed a David versus Goliath-style victory over supermarket giant Tesco.

Will Chase, a Herefordshire-based farmer who produces Tyrrells Potato Chips, said Tesco had been stocking his products - which retail at around 90p - despite his refusal to supply to the chain."

BBC, 2006

In 2008, I decided to sell Tyrrell's. The company was successful, but for it to grow, changes needed to be made in-house. During my final time at Tyrrell's, everybody told me that I needed more people, particularly at management level, so I went about hiring more staff, who then brought all their pals with them.

I'm not a corporate, and being at the helm of a large corporate structure never appealed to me. If I'm honest, I also didn't like the cost of having a large team. Expense accounts and car allowances. Meetings to schedule meetings. It all seemed so unnecessary, especially when our profits remained the same in spite of the fact that we were making and selling considerably more products. My management style now is the same as it was then – hire the right people, have meetings when they are necessary and let everybody get on and do their jobs. After all, we were making 30 per cent net profit.

I'd had many offers before, but the timing was right this time around and I sold the business to a venture capitalist. The reason I chose them? They offered me the most money and I was ready to walk away.

In hindsight, if it had been possible for me to easily get divorced at the time, I wouldn't have sold Tyrrell's. The factory still existed on the farm that I'd been born and raised and the whole company represented my life's work at the time. But as soon as I left, all sentimentality began to erode and I felt liberated to start a new chapter of my life with no regrets.

Yes, I could've just gone and retired, you've got to be happy, haven't you? If I didn't have the drive I wouldn't have had it in the first place. That was what brought me to my next challenge. I'd heard that Sidney Frank sold Grey Goose vodka and I thought 'wow, that's more exciting, that's more interesting if we could apply the pedigree to Gin and Vodka.'

RECIPES

Verzon House chef Callum McDonald shares some of his favourite food

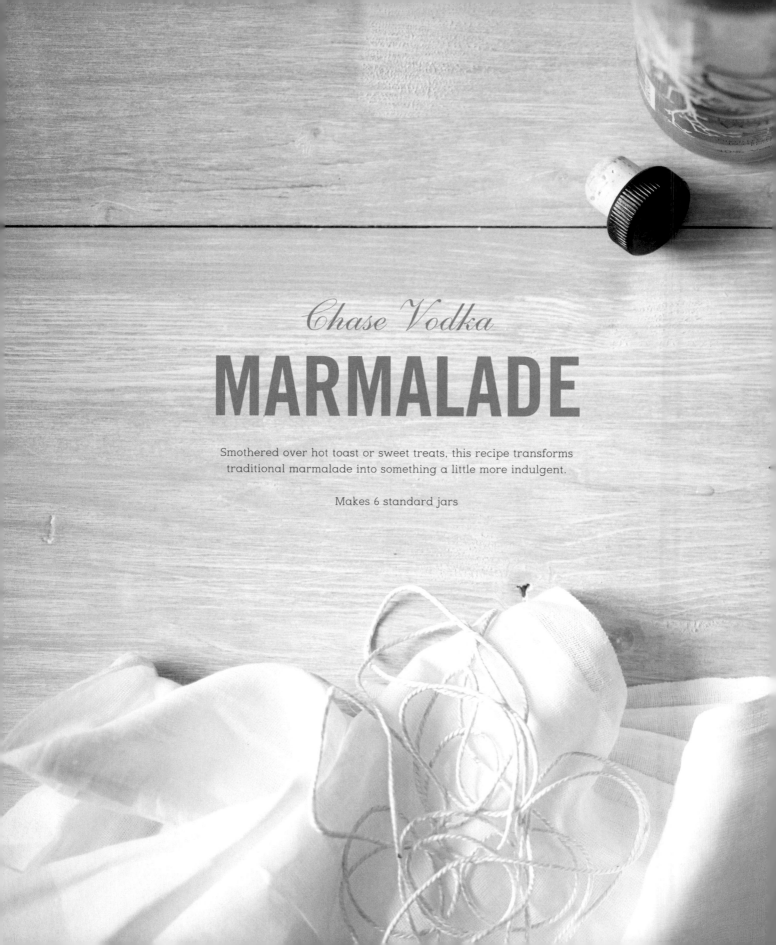

Chase Vodka

MARMALADE

Smothered over hot toast or sweet treats, this recipe transforms
traditional marmalade into something a little more indulgent.

Makes 6 standard jars

Chase Vodka Marmalade

YOU WILL NEED...

3 oranges
900g sugar
700ml Chase Vodka
6 sterilized jars

METHOD...

To begin, halve and juice the oranges. Scoop out the pulp and tie it up in a muslin cloth. Measure 1 litre of water into a bowl and add the vodka, the juice, shredded skin and wrapped pulp and leave to soak for 24 hours (this intensifies the flavour and reduces the cooking time).

When ready, place the ingredients, into a heavy-based pan. Bring the mixture to a gentle boil then turn down the heat and simmer for 2 hours, until the peel has become very soft. Carefully remove the muslin bag, allow to cool slightly, then return the contents to the mix.

There should now be 775g of mixture. If there is less, add water to make up the difference and then return the mix to the pan. Add the sugar and boil for 10 minutes. To check the marmalade is ready, take it off the heat and spoon a small amount onto a plate and put it in the freezer. After two minutes you should be able to push the marmalade from the freezer with your finger. If the surface wrinkles and it holds its form, then it's ready. If it doesn't, return the pan to the heat for two minutes and check again. Continue this process until it achieves the desired effect.

Once ready, carefully spoon the mixture into the jam jars, seal and leave to cool.

Treacle and Peanut

BREAD

This is comfort food at its best. We love it on a cold winter's day,
served with lashings of butter and our marmalade (see page 52).

Makes one large loaf

Treacle &
Peanut Bread

YOU WILL NEED...

10g fresh yeast (or 4g dried yeast)

20g natural yoghurt

25g treacle

100ml milk

100ml warm water

170g wholemeal flour

170g strong white flour

10g salt

10g butter, softened

50g dry roasted peanuts, chopped

METHOD...

In a bowl, combine the yeast, yoghurt, treacle, milk and water. Stir the mix and allow it to stand until you see bubbles (approximately 2 minutes). Put both flours in the bowl of an electric stand mixer and add the wet ingredients. Using the dough hook attachment, mix on a low speed for 15 minutes, then add the salt, butter and peanuts and mix for a further 5 minutes. Place the dough into an oiled bowl, cover with cling film and leave in a warm place to prove for 40 minutes.

Once proved, turn the dough onto a lightly floured surface and knead the air out of it. Then shape it into a small loaf, place onto a lightly floured tray, cover with a damp cloth and leave to prove for a further 50 minutes. If you have a trigger spray bottle handy, fill it with water and spray the dough every 10 minutes. Alternatively, sprinkle it with a little water using your fingers.

When the dough has finished proving, preheat the oven to 220°C and bake for 35-40 minutes, until crusty. To tell if your bread is ready, tap it on the bottom. If it gives off a hollow sound, remove from the oven and leave it to cool on a wire rack.

Rarebit and

CRISPY BACON

This recipe is a firm favourite at the Verzon.
Who doesn't love beer, cheese and bacon?

Rarebit &
Crispy Bacon

YOU WILL NEED...

55g butter
50g flour
200g ale
2 tsps Lea & Perrins
Worcestershire sauce
1 tsp English mustard
1 tsp Marmite
200g Hereford Hop cheese, or
mild cheddar, grated
2 egg yolks
8 rashers of bacon
4 slices of treacle and peanut
bread (see page 56), toasted

Ale Caramel
400ml ale
100g sugar

METHOD...

In a heavy-based pan, melt
the butter, add the flour and
mix thoroughly to form a thick
paste. Cook for a further minute,
continuously stirring. Gradually
add the ale, making sure it's fully
combined before you add any
more. Stir in the Worcestershire
sauce, mustard and Marmite.
Add the cheese. Once it's formed
a smooth mixture, pour into a
separate bowl and set aside.

Make the caramel by placing
the sugar and ale into a heavy-
based pan and stirring over a
medium heat. Once the sugar has
dissolved and the mixture has
reduced by two thirds, take off
the heat and leave to the side.

Lay the bacon on a grill tray and
cook until crispy.

Assemble the rare bit by
spreading the cheese mixture
onto the bread and placing it
under the grill until it's bubbling
and brown. Serve with a drizzle
of the ale caramel and top with
the crispy bacon.

Wye Valley

ASPARAGUS MOUSSE

WITH GOAT'S CHEESE, BEETROOT AND ONION CARAMEL

We developed this dish to showcase English asparagus – one of our country's finest vegetables. Yes, it's a little challenging, but definitely worth the effort.

Wye Valley
Asparagus Mousse

YOU WILL NEED...

125g asparagus, finely chopped
35g unsalted butter
30g spinach
20g cream
3 egg whites
1 gelatine leaf
1/2 tsp lemon juice
Salt to taste

Whipped goat's cheese
100g goat's cheese
75g double cream

Salt-baked beetroot
600g beetroot, washed
800g salt
60g water

Beetroot crisps
140g beetroot, washed
Olive oil
Salt

Onion caramel
1 small onion, sliced
100g sugar

To serve
8 asparagus spears
Peppery salad leaves
or watercress

METHOD...

To prepare the mousse, line 4 moulds with cling film and melt the butter in a pan over a medium heat. Add the asparagus, sprinkle with salt, cover and cook for 3-4 minutes, until the asparagus looks light in colour. Add the cream and cook for a further minute. Pour the mixture into a food processor, add the spinach and blend for a couple of minutes until smooth. Over a bowl, pass the mixture through a sieve and allow to slightly cool.

Add the gelatine to 100ml of water. In a small pan, bring 20ml of water to a simmer. When the gelatine has softened, squeeze the excess liquid from the sheets and add to the hot water. Take the pan off the heat, stir until the gelatine has dissolved and pour into a large bowl and set aside.

Add the lemon juice to the egg whites and whisk into soft peaks with an electric mixer. Fold the gelatine mixture through the asparagus purée. Once fully incorporated, carefully fold in half of the whipped egg white. Add the remaining egg whites and combine. Fill the moulds, smoothing the top with the back of a knife, cover with cling film and refrigerate for 3-4 hours, until set.

While waiting for the mousse to set, prepare the toppings. For the whipped goat's cheese, begin by breaking the cheese into small chunks, place it in a bowl, covering with cling film and setting it aside for 20 minutes. Once the cheese has reached room temperature, bring the cream to the boil in a heavy-based pan.

When ready, pour the cream over the goat's cheese and beat with a whisk until smooth. Scoop the mixture into a piping bag and leave it to one side.

For the salt-baked beetroot, preheat the oven to 170°C. In a bowl, combine the salt and water and then spoon half the mixture onto the bottom of a roasting tray. Top and tail the beetroot and place on the tray. Spoon the rest of the salt mix over the beetroot, moulding it around the vegetables to make a shell. Bake for 80 minutes. Remove from the oven and allow the beetroot to cool in the salt crust.

For the crisps, preheat the oven to 170°C and cut the beetroot into 2mm thick slices using a mandoline. Place the slices on a tray and lightly sprinkle with salt. After 10 minutes, the moisture from the beetroot will have seeped out. Using kitchen towel, pat the beetroot dry. Line a baking tray with greaseproof paper and lay the beetroot slices flat on top. Drizzle with olive oil and place another sheet of greaseproof paper over the beetroot. Bake for 20 minutes or until crisp. Set aside to cool.

To prepare the onion caramel, place the sugar and 20ml water into a heavy-based pan. Bring the mixture to the boil over a medium heat. After 3 minutes it should become a light golden colour. As soon as this colour is achieved, pour directly into a blender, add the onion and blend until smooth. Pour through a sieve into a small bowl and set aside to cool.

TO SERVE

Break the salt crust on the beetroot, rinse and remove the skin. With a sharp knife, cut each into 6 pieces and lay three on each plate as shown. Remove the moulds from the fridge and place one on each plate, cling film side up. Peel off the cling film and lightly blowtorch the side of the ring before lifting it off gently (use oven gloves as the ring will be hot). Pipe six little mounds of the whipped goat's cheese onto each plate. Balance two of the beetroot crisps on the mounds. Cut the blanched asparagus spears on an angle, drizzle with olive oil and carefully arrange around the mousse. Drizzle with the onion caramel and garnish with colourful peppery leaves or watercress. To make this dish especially decadent, top with truffle shavings.

Smoked Vodka

CURED SALMON

BUCKWHEAT BLINIS, HORSERADISH
CRÈME FRAÎCHE

This is our take on a classic. The vodka provides a subtle smokiness that is perfect when served with a smoky mary (see page 156). Bliss!

Smoked Vodka Cured Salmon

YOU WILL NEED...

450g salmon fillet, skin on
125ml Chase Smoked Vodka
132g Muscovado sugar
122g sea salt
Zest of half a lemon

Buckwheat blinis

500g butter, melted
300g buckwheat flour
300ml milk, lukewarm
8g dried yeast
4 tsp sugar
1 tsp salt
2 eggs, separated
1/2 tsp lemon juice
1 tsp horseradish, finely grated

Horseradish crème fraîche

40g double cream
30g horseradish, finely grated
200g crème fraîche
1 tsp lemon juice

METHOD...

To cure the salmon, start by scoring the skin at 1cm intervals. Cover a tray with cling film, place the salmon on the centre, skin side down. In a bowl, combine the smoked vodka, sugar, sea salt and lemon zest, and distribute evenly over the salmon. Wrap tightly with more cling film, ensuring there's no leakage, and refrigerate for three days.

On the day you're ready to serve, make the blinis. In a bowl, mix together the yeast, sugar and milk and leave to stand until it starts to bubble (approximately 2 minutes). In a separate bowl, mix together the flour, salt, egg yolks, lemon juice, horseradish and melted butter. Stir in the yeast mixture. Whisk the egg whites, until they form soft peaks, and fold through the batter. Cover the bowl in cling film and leave to prove for 30 minutes. When ready, remove the clingfilm and stir with a spoon to remove the air.

To cook the blinis, melt a knob of butter, along with a splash of oil, in heavy-based frying pan on a medium heat. Using a dessert spoon, carefully drop the batter onto the pan to form small blinis. Fry for 2 minutes on each side, until golden. Repeat until all the mixture has been used.

For the crème fraîche, put the horseradish and cream into a small saucepan. Bring the mixture to the boil and simmer until the cream has reduced by a half (approximately 1 minute). Pass the cream through a sieve over a bowl and mix in the crème fraîche and lemon juice. Season with salt and pepper and chill until ready to serve.

TO SERVE...

Unwrap the salmon and wash thoroughly with cold water. Pat the fillet dry with a tea towel, remove the skin and cut into 2cm slices, widthways. Arrange on a plate with a slice of the cured salmon on top of each blini. Add a dollop of the crème fraîche.

MINESTRONE

This is both a tasty recipe and fantastic way to use up leftover roast meat.

Serves 4

MINESTRONE

YOU WILL NEED...

1 sprig thyme leaves
100g butter
4 tsps rapeseed oil
2 garlic cloves
200g onion
150g turnip
150g carrot
150g celeriac
150g celery
150g parsnip
150g pearl barley, soaked
2 tsps tomato purée
1.5l lamb stock
300g lamb shoulder, diced (can
be left over from Sunday lunch
or fresh, if fresh, brown before
using.)
25g parsley, chopped

METHOD...

Dice all the vegetables into
1/2 cm pieces. Melt the butter
with the oil in a heavy-based
pan over a medium heat. Add
the thyme and allow to infuse
for 30 seconds. Add the diced
vegetables and season with salt
and pepper. Cover with a lid
and sweat until the vegetables
have softened, stirring
occasionally (approximately 10
minutes). Add the tomato purée,
pearl barley and lamb stock. If
using fresh lamb, add this now
too and simmer for 20 minutes,
until the pearl barley is tender
and the stock has thickened.
If using cooked lamb, add it
now and simmer for a further
five minutes. To finish, top with
parsley and serve.

Brixham
MUSSELS
WITH WILLY'S CIDER AND SAGE

This is a simple, yet flavourful recipe to try. Willy's adds the taste of Herefordshire countryside and brings the dish together splendidly.

Brixham Mussels

YOU WILL NEED...

1kg Brixham mussels, cleaned
and de-bearded
3 banana shallots, diced
3 cloves garlic, diced
12 large sage leaves, chopped
120ml Willy's Cider
50ml double cream
1/2 lemon, juiced
Olive oil

METHOD...

Place a heavy-based pan on a
high heat and add big glugs
of olive oil. Add the shallots
and garlic and stir until they
turn a light golden colour. Add
the mussels and the cider and
quickly cover the lid. After two
minutes, add the lemon juice,
sage and cream and season with
salt and pepper. Cover for a
further two minutes.

TO SERVE...

Split the mussels and the sauce
between four bowls and serve
with big chunks of crusty bread.

Braised

OX CHEEK

ROAST ONION, ROAST GARLIC MASH
PRUNE & ALE JUS

This dish really is worth the extra work. Try your best to source
Herefordshire beef, melts in the mouth.

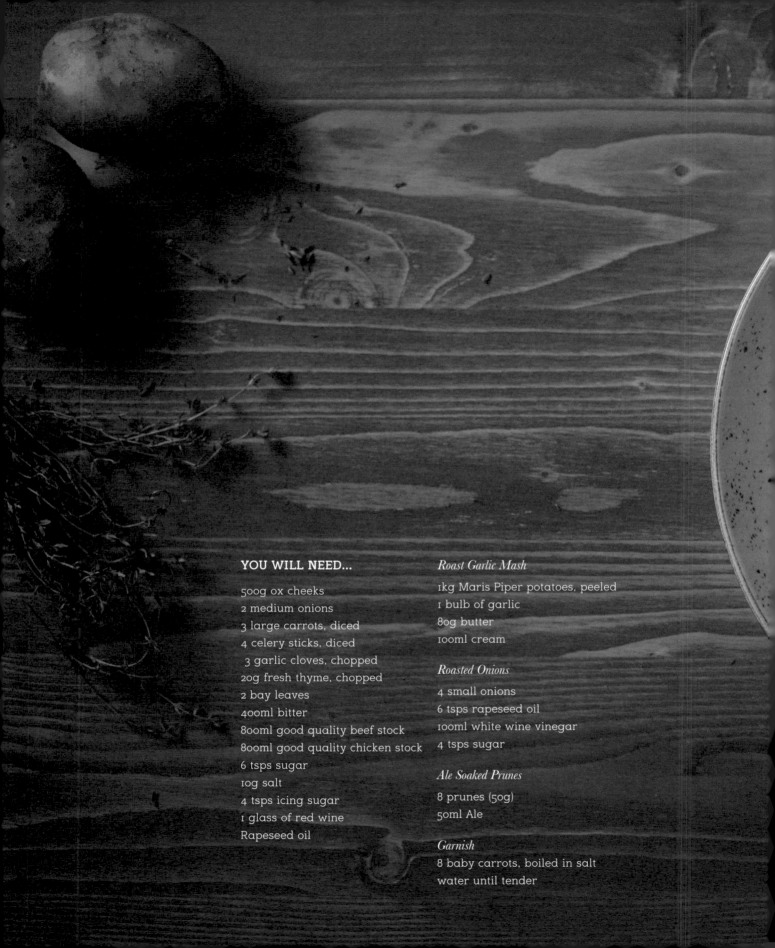

YOU WILL NEED...

500g ox cheeks
2 medium onions
3 large carrots, diced
4 celery sticks, diced
 3 garlic cloves, chopped
20g fresh thyme, chopped
2 bay leaves
400ml bitter
800ml good quality beef stock
800ml good quality chicken stock
6 tsps sugar
10g salt
4 tsps icing sugar
1 glass of red wine
Rapeseed oil

Roast Garlic Mash

1kg Maris Piper potatoes, peeled
1 bulb of garlic
80g butter
100ml cream

Roasted Onions

4 small onions
6 tsps rapeseed oil
100ml white wine vinegar
4 tsps sugar

Ale Soaked Prunes

8 prunes (50g)
50ml Ale

Garnish

8 baby carrots, boiled in salt
water until tender

METHOD...

In a pan, brown the ox cheeks in a little oil for 5-6 minutes per side until lightly coloured. Sprinkle with the icing sugar until sticky and caramelised. Remove from the pan and deglaze with the red wine, reducing it by three quarters. Remove from the pan and set aside.

Preheat the oven to 160°C. Dry the pan with kitchen towel, add a tablespoon of rapeseed oil and the vegetables and stir. After 10 minutes, add the garlic, thyme and bay leaves and cook for a further five minutes, stirring at minute intervals. Add both stocks, the bitter, sugar and salt. Bring to the boil and reduce liquid by two thirds. Pass the liquid through a sieve into an oven proof dish, add the browned ox cheeks, and cover with foil. Cook for 1 hour and 50 minutes.

For the roast garlic mash, preheat the oven to 160°C. Cut the top off the garlic, wrap it in foil and roast for 45 minutes. Cut the potatoes into golf ball-sized pieces, place in a pan with a teaspoon of salt and cover with water. Cook over a moderate heat, simmering the potatoes until a knife goes through them with no resistance. Drain and return the potatoes to the pan. Add the butter, cream and begin to mash. Once the desired consistency has been reached, squeeze the soft garlic into the mash and stir well. Season with salt and pepper.

Peel the onions, cut them in half from top to bottom and season with salt and pepper. Add the oil to an ovensafe frying pan and cook the onions over a medium heat, face down, for five minutes until dark. Add the sugar to the pan. Once it begins to caramelise, add the vinegar and reduce the mix by a third. Turn the onions upside down, cover with greaseproof paper and tin foil and cook in the 160°C preheated oven for 1 hour.

To make the prunes, warm the ale in a small pan, add the dried fruit, cover and leave to soak.

TO SERVE

Turn the oven to 180°C, uncover the ox cheeks and pick out the bay leaves. Remove half the liquid and strain into a small pan, add the prunes and simmer gently until warm. Spoon some of the remaining liquid over the cheeks and return to the oven for 8-10 minutes, basting every 2 minutes, until a deep, rich glaze is reached. To plate up, arrange the mashed potato, roasted onions and carrots on a plate and place one cheek on top. Spoon over the prunes and the sauce and serve.

White Chocolate

CHEESECAKE

WITH CHAMPAGNE-POACHED MIXED BERRIES AND RASPBERRY SORBET

These miniature cheesecakes are ideal for dinner parties or family lunches. They are easy to prepare and the Chase Raspberry Liqueur packs a fruity punch.

White chocolate cheesecake

YOU WILL NEED...

100g Hobnobs biscuits, crushed
35g butter, melted
90g white chocolate
140g cream cheese
50g icing sugar
45ml double cream, whipped

Jelly

90g Raspberries
50g Chase Raspberry Liqueur
5g Icing sugar
1 Gelatine leaf
10ml Water

Sorbet

500g raspberries
80g caster sugar
200ml Chase raspberry liqueur
150ml sugar syrup (100g sugar and 100g
water, boiled and reduced by a quarter)

Poached Berries

150g Mixed Berries
100ml Champagne
25g Caster Sugar

METHOD...

To make the cheesecake, start with the base. Preheat the oven to 100°C. In a bowl, mix together the melted butter and crushed Hobnobs. Split the mix between 4 individual metal ring moulds and press into the bottom to create a flat surface. Bake for five minutes and set aside to cool.

In a bowl, whisk together the icing sugar and cream cheese until smooth and shiny. Then melt the chocolate in a heatproof bowl over a pan of simmering water and add to the cream cheese mix. Gently fold in the whipped cream, split the mixture between the four moulds and refrigerate for at least 2 hours, until set.

Once the cheesecakes have set, make the jelly. Blend the raspberries, sugar and vodka together, pass the mix through a sieve then, over a low heat, warm the mixture to body temperature. Soak the gelatine in cold water until soft. Squeeze off the excess water and add to the raspberry mixture, stirring until completely dissolved. Pour over the four moulds and return to the fridge until set.

You can make the sorbet in advance. Place the raspberries and caster sugar in a saucepan, cover with a lid and gently simmer for two minutes. Remove the lid and simmer for a further two minutes to reduce the liquid. Blend and leave to cool. When ready, add the sugar syrup, raspberry mixture and vodka to an ice cream maker and churn until ready.

For the poached berries, begin by putting them in a bowl. Then add the champagne and sugar to a small saucepan and simmer over a medium heat until the sugar has dissolved and the liquid has reduced by a quarter. Pour the champagne mix over the berries, cover with cling film and leave to stand until cool.

TO SERVE

To remove the cheesecakes, warm the side of the metal ring with a blowtorch and carefully remove the ring (use oven gloves as the ring will be hot). Strain the liquid from the poached berries and lay on an angle, in a neat line in the centre of the plate. With an ice cream scoop ball the sorbet and place at the opposite side to the cheesecake. To finish, spoon a few drops of the champagne berry liquor around the plate and on top of the berries

Williams ~~GB~~ *Gin*

TRUFFLES

These truly decadent truffles should be reserved for
special occasions. Remember to share!

Makes 15

Gin Truffles

YOU WILL NEED...

130g Dark Chocolate
(30g grated for decoration)
120g Double Cream
25g Caster Sugar
13g Butter
30g Williams GB Gin

METHOD...

Break up 100g dark chocolate into small pieces, place in a bowl and set aside.

In a heavy-based pan on a medium heat, add 100mls of the cream, the butter and sugar. Once the mix has reached scalding temperature, pour over the chocolate.

Stir until fully incorporated then add the remaining cream and gin, mix thoroughly and refrigerate for 12 hours.

Remove from the fridge and shape into 15 equal size balls, roll in the grated chocolate until covered and place on tray lined with baking paper and return to the fridge

THE GREAT CHASE

Turning potatoes into vodka and gin

The Great Chase

My aim when starting Williams Chase was simple – to create a product of provenance and pedigree, which would change the way people drink white spirits.

When I started Tyrrell's, people thought I was mad, but I pressed on anyway. The public were interested in where their food had come from and I thought I could do the same with the white spirits world. I couldn't believe that the big spirits companies were making so much money producing alcohol from what is essentially neutral grain spirit (NGS). Unlike wine, people didn't seem to care where their white spirits came from and what they were made of, so I decided to see if I could change their minds – starting with Chase Vodka, which was followed quickly by Williams GB Gin – the product I'm most proud of to date.

I played around with making vodka a few years before I sold Tyrrell's. I'd had the idea after running into a group of rowdy Americans while in Barbados in 2004. We were all at the bar and I noticed them making their way through a big bottle of vodka and they offered me some.

If I'm being honest, I'd never been much of a vodka drinker. Whenever I tried it in the past, it tasted like nail varnish remover. In my mind, it was a cheap crass product that served a singular purpose – to get you drunk as quickly as possible.

I didn't, however, want to be rude to my new friends from across the pond, so I accepted their offer and was pleasantly surprised – it tasted fantastic and I asked to see the bottle. The vodka was made from potatoes and a new idea was born.

It was a back-burner notion to start with as I had my hands full with running Tyrrell's, but on a work trip back to the States a little while later, I noticed more potato vodka for sale and began looking into equipment suppliers in earnest. We made a couple of batches of Tyrrell's Vodka to start, but it was only once my time was freed up to pursue other projects that I started to think about building my own distillery.

Real vs Fake

While it's true that I probably could have afforded not to work after Tyrrell's, doing nothing has never been my style. If I was that kind of person, I would never have built my companies in the first place. I needed a new project and once again wanted to create something from scratch, to make a new product with provenance and pedigree that I could put my name on.

Not only could I make vodka and gin from my potatoes, but like chips, here was a product that was being made cheaply and mass-marketed by big companies for high returns. Why couldn't I apply the same artisan recipe that I had used to make Tyrrell's a success to do the same for white spirits? People care about where their wine is grown, the grape varieties, soil type and process, so why didn't they think the same way about their vodka and gin?

I'm really passionate about making everything from natural ingredients. The reason my vodkas and gins are special is because we make everything from our Herefordshire potatoes - hence the single-estate magic.

It would've been so much easier to do as all the other gin distilleries do – buy in the NGS, distill it, whack a label on it and then spend the money you've saved on a massive marketing campaign telling twee stories about the filtration or botanicals.

If all I was interested in was making money, then this would have been the sensible way to go, but doing that would go against everything I believed in. I wanted to celebrate Herefordshire and all it had to offer by doing something unique and respected. In theory, this was great, but we almost created a handicap for ourselves as wanting to control the entire process made it very expensive for us to make. Luckily we've stuck to our guns and we've managed to create exactly what I set out to do.

Building the distillery at Rosemaund Farm, 2008

The set up

In many ways, setting up Williams Chase was similar to the early days of Tyrrell's. Potatoes were our raw product and we were once again going to make something authentic. I was on a steep learning curve and needed to find the equipment and staff to help me.

In the last few years, there's been a proliferation of small distilleries, but when I was setting up mine in 2007, customs law dictated that I needed a 2,000 litre still and a massive rectifying column. The law was changed the year after, which is why there are now a lot of so called 'artisan' gin and vodka makers, but fortunately I had to go big or go home. I think that if I'd been setting it up under the new laws, there's a possibility that I would've kept making vodka and gin as a hobby instead of building Williams Chase into what it is today – the first and only single-estate vodka and gin distillery in Britain.

Left over from the Tyrrell's factory, we already had a
potato handling line, peeler, and a set of shiny tanks
that could ferment up to 100 tonnes of potatoes. The rest
of the equipment we sourced from all over the world,
most notable of which is our rectifying column. Standing
at 80ft (the largest in Europe) and affectionately known
as Tall Jimmy, this piece of kit is now as iconic as it is
useful. We also opted for a completely manual system
as this allows us more control over the entire distilling
process – from seed to bottle.

We found the perfect place to set up – Rosemaund Farm
near Preston Wynne in Herefordshire. The building
that houses our distillery was once an experimental
hop drying kiln built in the 1950s when agriculture was
getting a lot of support from the government to feed
the growing population after the war. It had long been
disused when I stumbled upon it, but with its glazed loft
and location, it was the perfect place for me to build a
distillery. Getting planning permission was a bit of a
headache because we needed to make sure there was
enough space for Tall Jimmy, but everything was finally
put in place and we were ready to make our first batch.

Tim and Joe preparing the gin botanicals

The early days

At the beginning, it was just five of us who were the original 'distillers'. I'd done a course in the US, but mostly we learnt on the job. We quickly discovered that turning potatoes into vodka was a totally different process than turning them into chips. At Tyrrell's, the work was hard, but for the distillery only the initial stages were the same. We still had to wash and prepare the spuds, but that's where the similarities ended - and this was to be a whole new adventure.

The biggest initial surprise was how long the distilling process took. From start to finish, it takes 5-6 weeks to make our vodka and another week longer for our gin (which is made from our vodka). We mashed huge quantities of potatoes, had to wait two weeks for them to ferment and be distilled, only to receive a small quantity of spirit. It was a big shock to discover that 12 tonnes of spuds made only a few litres of vodka. This is why nobody else makes their own base spirit.

One of the amazing things we did learn, however, was that we didn't need to filter or add anything to our vodka after it came out of the rectifier. We were able to produce a 100% natural product without needing additives. All we had to do was add water from our own springs. I'd succeeded with what I planned to do and it felt – and tasted - great.

What's in a name?

I could've kept the name Tyrrell's for the vodka, but there's a wine maker in Australia called Murray Tyrrell who had registered the name globally for alcohol, and while he said he was happy for us to use it (as long as we sent him a case a year), I wanted to own the brand outright and was proud enough of our product to want to put my name on it too.

Chase Manhattan bank in the US, weren't too happy about it. We did get a letter from them saying that they were going to sue us if we didn't change the name, but we wrote back saying that we weren't going to budge and we never heard from them again. It wasn't quite the same as the Tesco David and Goliath story, but I'm proud of it nonetheless.

I kept the name Chase for the vodka, but for the gin I called it Williams – my mother's maiden name. It makes me proud to see my family name on our products. As a small family business, I think it's important to put your name on something you truly believe in. It's the highest sign of respect. If you are proud of it, put your name on it.

And, if I look back at many successful brands of the past, most had their family name on them. It's an endorsement by the founder and, I think, adds an extra guarantee that no corners have been cut in production.

I believe if you are proud of it, put your name on it

Voted the World's best tasting vodka, by the San Francisco World Spirit Awards

Potato harvest, 2008

The single-estate process

Everything that has been made by us at Williams Chase has been done with 100 per cent respect and passion. The process is time consuming, but my goal has always remained the same. No corners can be cut – period. There is a finite number of bottles we can make in a year, which is why we make sure that everything we produce is the best that Herefordshire can offer, as it's a small batch process and I wish to keep it that way.

It took us a while to refine the process. But in the end I think we got it right. In 2010 our Chase Vodka won the world's best vodka award at the San Francisco World Spirits Competition. I can't overstate how huge this was for us. We were only just starting out. In fact, the day that it was announced that we had won, we were in the process of moving our offices out of my farmhouse and into our new digs on Rosemaund Farm. As a result, we were disconnected from our emails for three days, but did the best we could. We did make it onto Sky and the BBC in the UK and on Fox and CNBC in the States, the latter of which was great even though we didn't have a distributor in the US at the time. For me it was a vindication. A lot of the naysayers when I first started Williams Chase thought I couldn't pull it off, but I knew that I had made a quality product and the award helped me prove it.

And it's the taste of our Chase Vodka and our Williams GB Gin that people are really starting to appreciate. Because our vodka is only made from two ingredients – potatoes and spring water – it's a pure, clean alcohol that can be enjoyed on its own. We run tours through our distillery and our visitors most often comment on the taste – particularly the fact that it doesn't need the addition of mixers and such to be drinkable.

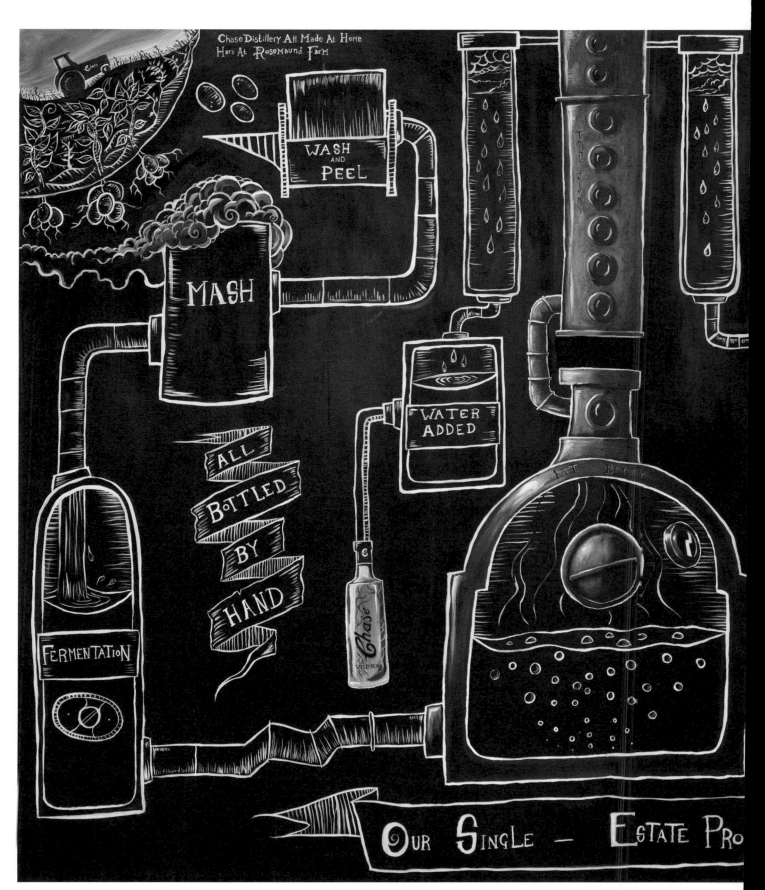

Illustration by Tom Roberts

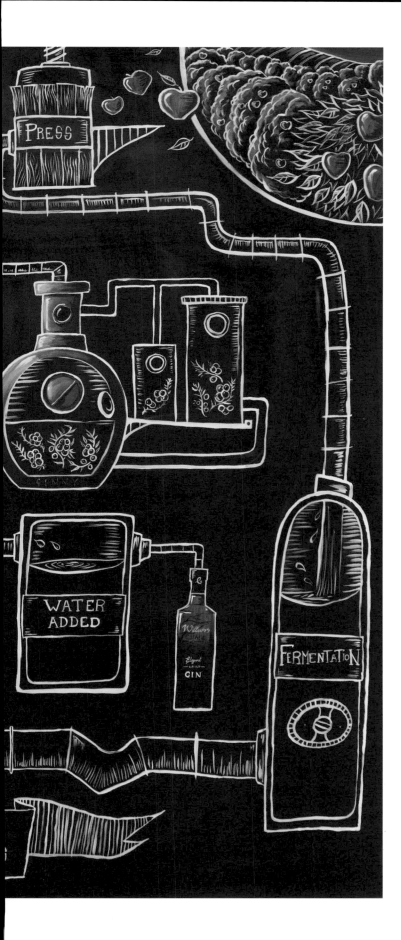

Gin is made from vodka

They're also surprised to learn that gin is made from vodka. We actually worked with our Spanish customers to come up with the perfect recipe for our Williams GB Extra Dry Gin. I'm not going to let you in on all my secrets, but we found the magic by adding both juniper buds and berries in with the rest of our specially selected botanicals. My GB is an everyday gin perfect for a gin and tonic – and it's without a doubt the best thing that I've ever made from potatoes. The two years that it took to perfect the recipe were definitely worth it.

Raffy and the masher

The one that got away

Mashing

The first stage of the vodka making process is to convert the potatoes into sugars. The potatoes that we grow on the farm are old fashioned high starch varieties such as Lady Claire and Lady Rosetta. They are harvested in late summer and stored in wooden boxes for the rest of the year.

We tip them out of the boxes and into a water bath. Any stones that might be mixed in with them sink to the bottom, but the potatoes float and are drawn off into the peeling machine. The peel is mainly fibre and cannot be fermented, so we take it off and spread it on the fields as compost.

The naked potato that we are left with is basically starch and water. We mash them and heat them up to produce a runny mashed potato. This cooks the starch so that the enzymes can get to work, but because they are destroyed by heat, we have to cool the mash to 60°C before we can add them. After half an hour if you stick your finger in and taste it, it's already quite sweet. For the technically minded, what's happening is that the enzymes are breaking down the long chain starch molecules into simple sugars like maltose. These are what we can ferment to make alcohol. We keep cooling to around 30°C at which point we can add the yeast.

Lady Rosetta potatoes are perfect for distilling

Fermentation

This is one of our favourite bits. Not only are we making alcohol, but we don't actually have to do any work - the yeast does it all for us. The yeast starts to feed on the sugars that we have made out in the mash vessel and starts to reproduce.

This process has three waste products: firstly alcohol, which is a good thing and is what we are after, but also lots of carbon dioxide gas which makes the mash froth up and overflow if we're not careful, and lastly heat. We keep it cool at first to keep the rate of fermentation under control and after a week or so end up with a potato wine of between 8 and 10 per cent alcohol. Even I admit that it does not look or taste nice, but if we have done a good job and not put the yeast under any stress, we will have produced lots of good quality alcohol.

Olly Smith

Fat Betty, our copper batch pot

Our distiller, Emily

Distillation

The first distillation run is called a stripping run and we are not trying to do anything clever with the alcohol, but simply extract as much as possible from what we have fermented. The still, like our product, is handmade. It is completely copper which helps produce a smoother distillate by removing sulphates (and cyanide too if we ever start distilling cherries). It looks like something Jules Verne might have written about, especially when it's bubbling away and with the old-fashioned hand controlled steam valves. It's more than just a machine, its got soul and a character of its own. We have to do several stripping runs to empty the fermentation vessels and we end up with what are called 'low wines' at around 45-50 per cent ABV.

Rectification

This is where it starts to get complicated. The 'low wines' still don't taste very nice. This is because they are made up of lots of different substances in addition to the ethanol that we want. As well as not tasting good, some of the substances, such as methanol, can make you go blind so we need to remove these as well as concentrate the alcohol, which we do using our rectification column. This is over 80ft tall and extends up through the ceiling, up through the floor above and into a tower that we had to build on the roof of the distillery. Again it is all hand made from copper and looks stunning. We put the 'low wines' back into the pot still and heat them up again.

The vapour then passes up the rectification column through 42 bubble plates all the way to the top where we have a condenser with lots of cold water running through it. This condenses the alcohol vapour making it trickle all the way back down to the bottom of the column leaving a thin layer of liquid on each bubble plate before it runs back into the still to be re-boiled, re-evaporated and sent back around the loop again. As the vapour passes up the rectification column again, this time it is forced into the layer of liquid on each bubble plate. As a vapour entering a liquid it will naturally condense, but because energy cannot be created or destroyed, something has to give, and so something also has to evaporate from the layer of liquid, and because alcohol has a lower boiling point than water, it tends to be the alcohol that evaporates preferentially. We told you it was complicated, but the result is that as the vapour passes up through these bubble plates it gets progressively purer and purer, in other words it is getting more concentrated.

We run this like this for a couple of hours, with a lot of reflux condensation at the top of the column. This has the effect of concentrating the methanol at the top of the column because it has the lowest boiling point of any of the alcohols, so when we eventually reduce the amount of reflux and allow the alcohol to escape from the top of the column, the first bit that comes through is rich in methanol and can be separated off and collected in a tank. This has quite a strong chemical smell at first, but then when most of the methanol has come through it starts to be mixed with ethanol (the good alcohol that we want) and the smell reduces. We take samples here and sniff very carefully until we are certain that the methanol has all gone and at this point make a "cut" and send the product into a separate tank. If we have done a good job with the fermentation, this now makes up the bulk of the run and we can sit back for the next few hours just monitoring the process (or get on with some bottling or paperwork).

Through the windows at each bubble plate we can see the alcohol boiling away at around 80°C, and after quite some time, the first clue that we are nearing the end of the run comes when the temperature reading on the gauge at the bottom of the rectification column suddenly starts to increase. This shows that the ethanol has now all gone from the pot and higher alcohols, aldehydes, ketones and water are all starting to come through. We continue to monitor the process and watch as the temperature rises up the column as the ethanol escapes through the top and eventually we make a second "cut" collecting the last of the distillate in a third tank. We therefore have three different parts: the heads, which is basically methanol, the hearts, which is the ethanol we are after, and the tails, which is everything else. The hearts are concentrated to above 90 per cent ABV after this first rectification run.

For our second rectification run, our third distillation run in total, we take just the hearts and repeat the entire process ending up with a pure spirit at above 96 per cent ABV. Again we take care to keep as much of the character of the product as possible.

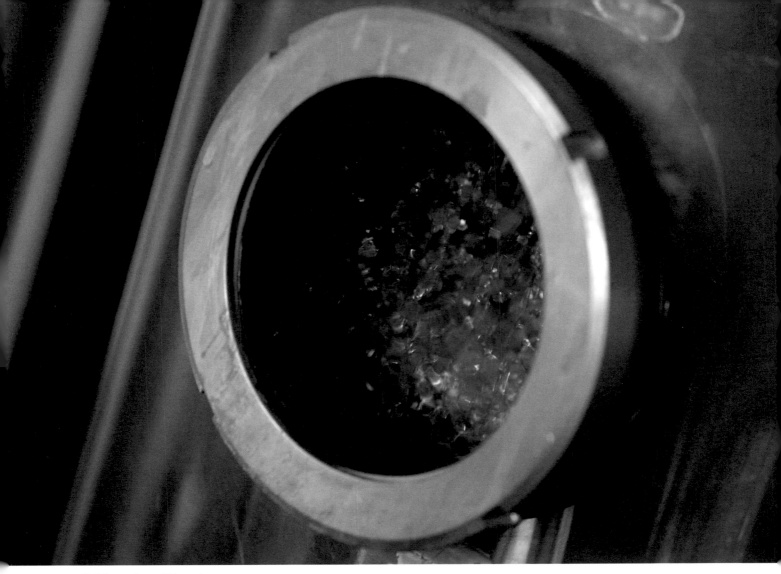

Tall Jimmy, the rectifying column

Head Distiller, Jamie Baggott

Finishing

Our product is designed to be drunk neat, and usually straight from the freezer, although we like to drink it at room temperature as you can pick up more of the subtleties of the flavour. We therefore need to do a bit of work to finish the spirit. Finally, we dilute it with water to 40 per cent ABV. The water comes from the aquifer underneath our orchard at the bottom of the valley.

Olena on the capping machine

Magda, hand bottling

Bottling

This is all done by hand. The bottles come into us with
the design already printed. We put them upside down
onto a turntable, which rinses them out. We then put
them on a basic but accurate filler which fills the bottle
to the required level. We put a cork in using a rubber
mallet and a strip or capsule over the top. We have to
put a little round duty stamp sticker on every bottle
and then it's ready for dispatch.

Creating our gin

After all the work to make our vodka - the base spirit for our gin - this is a really simple process. We start by opening the belly of our 250l Carter head style still, Ginny, we add in the Chase Vodka at 96 per cent ABV along with the same amount of water from the farm and a certain amount of junipers to marinade. The other botanicals are gathered into a pillowcase and placed into the carter head, where the flavours are infused into the vapours passing through. This method provides a very floral style with great length and depth - it has worked so well that we haven't had to change the recipe for four years. We believe in our GB gin so much that we've never entered it into any competitions – people are discovering and enjoying it all on their own.

Juniper berries

Joe and Ginny, Britain's first gin still for over 200 years

Design

I have done a lot of work over the years to make our bottles stand out on the shelves. I wanted our design to tell the story, and just as modern screen printing was good for Tyrrell's, I wanted to use the same for the spirits. We put the potato roots on the bottle to show where our vodkas and gins come from and added our story too. Then due to the popularity of the union flag we made the dickie-bows that we put on our bottlenecks. They're great fun and have made us instantly recognisable.

I used to worry when our competitors copied our designs. It started happening at the very beginning of Tyrrell's when a competitor put a celebrity on a tractor not long after we'd done the same thing. It took me a while to realise that it was far better for them to be doing something you'd already thought of. It's much better to lead than to follow.

We begin by distilling a single batch of gin using our fine potato vodka as a base spirit and our carefully selected choice of botanicals. Then we introduced our wild Herefordshire sloes and fresh mulberries and age it in oak barrels to create a unique batch of single-estate sloe gin. If something is worth doing, it is worth doing properly.

James, me and Harry, 2015

Me and my wife Kate, 2011

Family business

Starting the distillery also gave me the opportunity to work with my two eldest sons. Harry and James grew up as I built Tyrrell's, and now they're old enough (and willing!) to work with me. Both come with their own strengths. Harry runs his own farm and grows our potatoes, while James is our Chase Vodka brand ambassador and also manages international sales.

It's great to see them in the business, but I still want them to do their own things as it's much more satisfying building something from scratch. Harry is doing his own thing with his farm, while James also owns a pub in London with his friend Dom and is always looking at creating other businesses.

It's not just about potatoes

A couple of years ago, I moved to our new farm near Ledbury in Herefordshire, which came with 300 acres of cider apple orchards. They're beautiful trees that range in age from 70 to 200 years. The apples are all different cider apple varieties, including Michelin, Harry Masters, Dabinett and some ancient kinds that nobody knows the names of anymore.

And me, being the ever-curious type who is always hatching up new plans, wanted to see if I could make vodka and gin out of apples too. The gin, which is called Williams Elegant, is extremely complicated to make. The cider apples are small and bitter sweet with high tannins in the skin that give it a sophisticated fruity taste.

Elegant Gin is created by first pressing cider apples, fermenting the juice to create our Willy's Cider (some of which we bottle), then distilling it into Naked Chase Apple Vodka. To convert the Naked Chase into our Elegant Gin, we distil the spirit with 11 wild botanicals, including juniper, angelica, orange and lemon peel, hops and elderflower, in Ginny. The process is finished by the addition of naturally pure water taken from the aquifer that runs underneath the orchards on the farm. The resultant flavour is a full bodied, sharp yet fruity gin with tears and true provenance. It's a complex and labourious process that I use in my favourite cocktail – an Elegant Gin Martini (p.184)

Whisky is a passion too

Whisky is made from beer just as gin is made from vodka.

I had the idea to make whisky a year after building the distillery. I was at a trade show in Japan and they were showing some of the most respected whiskys in the world.

During my research, I discovered that whiskys are only taken seriously after they've been aged for ten years while it takes between 15 and 20 to find the real magic. Yes, it's a long-term project, but it's one that I'm very excited about.

Our whisky is five years old now. We made it by fermenting local Herefordshire Maris Otter barley into a beer wash and then distilling it three times in Fat Betty to retain the correct properties. I also wanted to retain a bit of the fuggles hops as I'm not making Whisky in Scotland and I wanted to add some of our local character to the finish.

Once the spirit was distilled, it was time to begin the ageing process – this is where the real magic happens. For the first two years, I used Bourbon barrels and left them in the loft above the distillery where there are extreme temperature fluctuations. I'd picked up the barrels from a very unique, small distillery somewhere in the world in 2005 and finally had a use for them.

Aging the whisky above the distillery has led to some quite interesting discoveries. Normally when whisky is aged between eight and ten years, you can expect around 10-15 per cent evaporation. This is known as the 'angel's share'. With our method, however, we expect to lose up to 60 per cent, so what we are left with is condensed into a very fine spirit.

We transferred the spirit into Olorosso sherry casks, which were supplied to us by the Domecq family in Jerez – a fifth generation father and daughter business that supplies the finest casks

The Domecq Family

to distillers all over the world. The whisky then spends 2-3 years here before being transferred into amphora clay pots from Tuscany – these are the same vessels we use at our vineyard in Provence (but more about that later).

Once the whisky is around ten years old, we'll bottle it and allow it to rest for a another few years, allowing it to mellow further. Yes, it's labourious and time and cash consuming, but the whisky is already showing promise and it's totally unique to our distillery.

Due to restrictions on time, availability of the perfect beer, the limited space we have in the loft and the massive amount we lose due to evaporation, it makes the process extreme and we'll not know the results until 2020, but my first barrels are five years old as I write this book and it's tasting good so far.

I'm calling the whisky's Will's Story as when it's ready to drink I would have been in business for 40 years and it represents my journey. Often whisky makers are rushing to get theirs to market within five years, but I've got a good feeling that this will be worth the wait. I might sell a few pre-release bottles are long as they're not opened until 2020!

HEREFORDSHIRE

Celebrating our home and England's most unspoilt county

Harvesting Dabinett apples

Our herd of Hereford cattle at home in Ledbury

Herefordshire

My home county is actually the biggest and most special star in this book. Not only was I born and raised at Tyrrells Court near the village of Dilwyn, it is also where I built my businesses.

But that is all about me – what makes it such a secret and special place is its beauty and serenity. Not many people from the outside know where it is – we're not on the commuter belt and The Cotswolds and Gloucesterhire nearby tend to take all the glory. Whenever I go to London and people ask me where I'm from, they've heard of Hereford, the county's capital, but would struggle to place it on a map.

All this makes Herefordshire unspoilt, undeveloped, natural, beautiful and quiet. For better (I think), the county has escaped a huge influx of new blood and keeps itself intentionally below the radar, bar for a few noteworthy exceptions. We're proud to host the annual Hay Literary Festival, but there are concerns that revelers will see how pretty it is here and want to come and join us. The secret might be out!

Despite our air of mystery, we are home to quite a few things
worthy of a mention. The Hereford beef breed, for example, and
the Mappa Mundi (the largest medieval map known to exist)
is kept in the Hereford Cathedral. Until a few years ago, the
county was the cider capital of the world too with Bulmers and
Westons putting us on the map. When the cider works was still
in the centre of Hereford, the whole city used to smell like the
beverage from September to November as the farmers carted
their tractor loads of apples to the site. Hereford is one of the
last big English cities to retain its rural community status.

And then, of course, there are now the potatoes, though this is a
relative new occurrence mainly as a result of the supermarkets
in the 90s wanting to sell pretty vegetables. The crops were
planted in Herefordshire's virgin soils to satisfy the demand
as traditional potato growing areas had contracted soil-borne
diseases which made their crops ugly. These days, the boom
has finished, so there are fewer potato farmers in The Shire - so
called as Herefordshire was the inspiration for J.R.R. Tolkien's
The Hobbit as it is so green and lush.

Herefordshire is also home to our very own Verzon House - the restaurant with rooms we own near Ledbury. The building was once a very famous farmhouse that had been a pub and a restaurant before we took it over. Now people come the world over to eat Callum's food (see his recipes from p.53) and to drink our spirits - and our wine (but more on that next time).

COCKTAILS

James Chase shares his favourite serves using our gins and vodkas

Chase Smoked Vodka

BLOODY MARY

This is Will's favourite and the perfect start to any morning. It's as personal as you can get: spicy or not, it's a great recipe to build on.

Chase
Smoked Vodka
Bloody Mary

YOU WILL NEED...

2 shots of Chase Smoked Vodka

4 shots of tomato juice

1/2 shot freshly squeezed lemon juice

8 drops of Tobasco Sauce

4 dashes of Worcestershire Sauce

2 grinds of black pepper

1 pinch of celery salt

Grated fresh horseradish to taste

METHOD...

Add all ingredients into a tumbler, mix,
then add lots of ice. Pour into a glass
and garnish with a celery stalk, slice of
lemon and pinch of black pepper.

JAMES TOP TIP...

For extra kick, add in one teaspoon of
freshly-grated horse radish.

Skinny

CHASE

At the pub, I've learnt that people are becoming more health
conscious and this serve has really shot to fame.

Skinny Chase

YOU WILL NEED...

2 shots Chase Vodka
Squeeze of half a lemon
Dash of citrus bitters (we love grapefruit)
Soda water

METHOD...

Pour the ingredients into a tumbler, fill with lots
of ice and top with soda water. Garnish with
a lime wedge.

Elegant

GIN FIZZ

This is our take on the Ramos gin fizz and one of
my personal favourites.

Elegant Gin Fizz

YOU WILL NEED...

1 shot Elegant Gin
1/2 shot freshly squeezed lemon juice
1/2 shot freshly squeezed lime juice
3/4 sugar syrup (2 sugar to 1 water mix)
1 fresh egg white
1 shot single cream

METHOD...

Dry shake all ingredients in a cocktail shaker

Shake hard again with lots of ice

Strain into a chilled glass with no ice and top with soda water.

Garnish with a thin slice of apple on the top.

Smoked Espresso

MARTINI

This is a great way to kick your evening into gear.
The smoked vodka really makes it sing.

Smoked Espresso Martini

YOU WILL NEED...

1 1/2 Shot Chase Smoked Vodka

1 1/2 shot (we love coffee from Cornwall Roaster Origin Coffee)

1/2 shot runny honey

A pinch of coarse sea salt.

METHOD...

Add ingredients into a cocktail shaker, Stir until the honey is dissolved.

Shake hard with ice

Strain into a chilled coupe glass, garnish with three coffee beans floating on the top

Did you know...

The exact history of the espresso martini is not known, but one theory suggests that the drink was first created by cocktail guru Dick Bradsell in 1984, which makes it a relative newcomer in cocktail making terms. Apparently a famous model came into Fred's bar and asked him to make her a drink that would 'wake me up and then f*** me up,' and the espresso martini was the result.

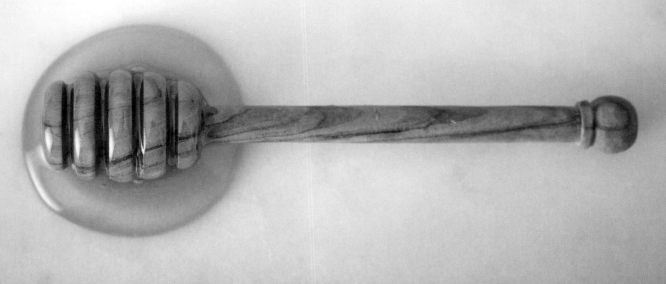

Marmalade

SOUR

This is such an easy serve and the
perfect start for any dinner party.

Marmalade Sour

YOU WILL NEED...

2 shots Chase Marmalade Vodka
1 shot freshly squeezed lemon juice
1/2 fresh egg white
3 dashes of angostura bitters

METHOD...

Shake all ingredients with Ice and strain
into a chilled martini glass

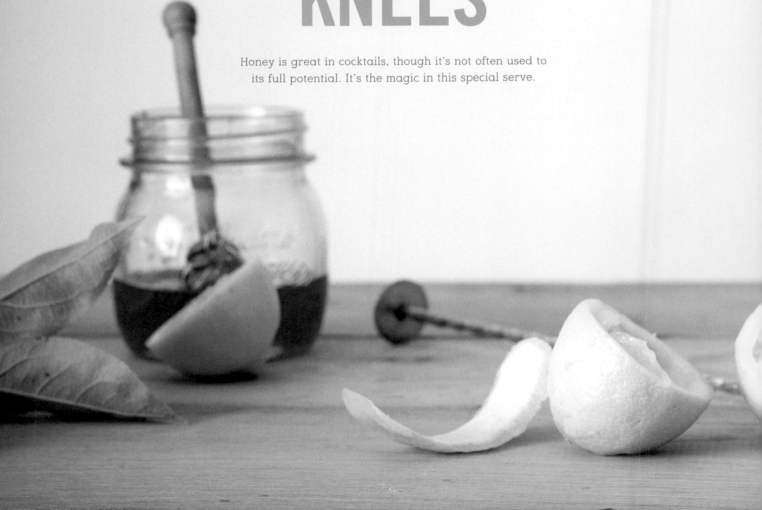

Bee's

KNEES

Honey is great in cocktails, though it's not often used to
its full potential. It's the magic in this special serve.

Bee's Knees

YOU WILL NEED...

2 shots Williams GB Gin
3 tspns of runny honey
1 shot freshly squeezed lemon juice

METHOD...

Shake all ingredients with ice, strain into a
chilled coupe glass.

JAMES' TOP TIP...

Twist lemon peel over the top for the drink to
take on just the smell of the essential oils - whip
the peel over the base of the glass too!

Royal
JAM

This cocktail was created by Tristan Stephenson to celebrate
the wedding of Prince William and Kate Middleton in 2011.
We've been serving it ever since.

Williams

Elegant
— CRISP —
GIN

GROWN,
DISTILLED AND BOTTLED
IN HEREFORDSHIRE,
ENGLAND

48% VOL 70CL ℮

Royal Jam

by Tristan Stephenson co-owner of
The Whistling Shop cocktail bar in
London and Fluid Movement.

YOU WILL NEED...

1 shot Williams Elegant Gin
1/2 shot freshly squeezed lemon juice
1/4 shot sugar syrup
2 barspoons English Strawberry conserve
5 drops Bob's Lavender Bitters
1/2 shot NyeTimber English sparkling wine

METHOD

Shake everything, but the sparkling wine, with ice,
strain into a teacup. Top up with English sparkling
wine.

When we serve this drink, we fill a decorative teapot
with 20g dry ice and 400ml of hot Earl Grey tea for an
amazing olfactory experience. It's a great one to try!

Williams

Elegant

— CRISP —

GIN

GROWN,
D AND **BOTTLED**
EFORDSHIRE,
NGLAND

VOL 70CL e

Great Chase

MARTINI

Our take on the classic cocktail.

Great Chase Martini

METHOD

Pour a dash of vermouth in to the bottom of an iced martini glass. Roll around glass and flick out excess.

Top with Chase Vodka or Williams Elegant Gin straight from the freezer. Garnish with a twist of lemon for the vodka or a slice of apple for the gin.

Did you know...

Dukes Hotel was a favourite of James Bond author Ian Fleming and is said to be the inspiration for the classic line 'shaken, not stirred'

Alessandro also invented the White Truffle Martini using white truffles from Alba in Italy, which takes three weeks to infuse. The recipe uses dry vermouth, Chase Vodka and a cheese-stuffed olive that has been marinated in homemade truffle vodka. It's delicious, but might be a bit difficult to make at home.

Alessandro Palazzi of Dukes Hotel

Marmalade Five

By Dom Jacobs, my friend and co-owner of The Running Horse in London

YOU WILL NEED...

2 shots Chase Marmalade Vodka
Fresh Strawberries
Blackberries
1 shot champagne

METHOD

Add the fruit, ice and vodka into a shaker.

Shake hard.

Double strain into a chilled coupe glass and top with Champagne.

Garnish with fresh cranberries, balancing on side of glass.

I first met Dom during one of our distillery tours in 2010. He was managing a bar in Leeds at the time and was totally engaged with what we were doing at Chase. We remained friends and when we found ourselves both living in London a little while later, we would often catch up and chat about what our dream bar would look like - and in 2013 we made it a reality. We re-opened The Running Horse, Mayfair's oldest pub, and the following year we launched The Whip - a small cocktail bar hidden upstairs that is also a great home away from home for Chase.

James Chase

HOW I FOUND THE MAGIC

My road to success

How I found the magic

The road to building a brand is different for everybody. All I can do is tell you what I've learnt along the way.

FIND YOUR EUREKA IDEA

Difficult to say, hard to do. Everybody who wants to work for themselves is looking for that widget, that one thing that will make them stand out from the pack. My initial idea to start Tyrrell's came from experience – identifying the gap and then having the guts and the belief in yourself to go for it so you have to be in it to win it.

RISK EVERYTHING

Profit is risk's reward – so the bigger the risk, the bigger the profit.

Everybody wants to get in on a good idea once somebody else has done all the hard work. To be one step ahead you have to be the one to risk it all. Are you hungry and desperate enough to make your business work? Will you put your house on the line to fund your idea? Will you give up on time with your children and family to make sure everything is running to the max?

I did a talk at a large university and the senior lecturer asked the audience who wanted to be an entrepreneur and all 400 students put their hands up. I then asked who would be prepared to give up their weekends and holidays, work 18 hours a day for seven days a week, invest all of their savings, and be prepared to borrow money all to make sure that their businesses were successful, and only a few hands remained in the air.

It's not easy, but you're only rewarded if you take a risk.

DON'T GO TO BED WITH PEOPLE YOU WORK WITH

I say this metaphorically, but now that I've got your attention what I mean is don't get too familiar with employees, partners and anyone else you do business with. Respect is important, but in my experience you can only have one strong boss who sets the direction. I've made the mistake many times of hiring people who I've got close to only to have them take me for granted.

IF IN A HOLE, STOP DIGGING

This is self-explanatory. Recognise when something isn't working and change direction as soon as possible.

Nothing ever stays the same. Your market might like vodka one day and gin the next. During my career I've seen supermarkets go from squeezing suppliers to becoming more socially aware, which I've had to work my various businesses around.

And if you're doing something and it's not working, be willing to change it. You might think your widget is going to change the world, but if it's not selling, it's time to tweak it or move onto something else. Don't be precious.

EMPLOY THE RIGHT PEOPLE

There are three things I look for in my employees: charisma, drive and intellect, the latter being the most important – and I'm not just talking about exam results. Often, the best people to take on are those who have had a rough time in life or done something extreme somewhere along the way and they'll do anything they need to and they also know how to encourage others.

You can tell when people are driven. At Tyrrell's, a young guy wrote to me many times wanting a sales job. He was told repeatedly that we didn't have any openings, but that didn't stop him. On a Tuesday not long after, he turned up unannounced with a coffee as a peace offering. I didn't take the meeting. The next day he bought a coffee and a newspaper, but I still didn't have the time. On the third day, he added a Danish pastry to the list. We met, and as I only employ people if I like them, he got the job.

NEVER BE JEALOUS OF THE COMPETITION WHEN THEY COPY YOU

I've had crisp and super-premium vodka brands copy my marketing ideas a number of times. It used to annoy me, but now I only really start to worry if they do things we've NOT thought of.

Creative meeting, 2014

IF IT SOUNDS TOO GOOD TO BE TRUE, THEN IT USUALLY IS

This is a great saying that I've held with me all of my life. Nothing is ever as easy or as profitable as it sounds.

MAKE YOUR OWN LUCK

Every success story has come about, to some degree, as a result of luck – but you can make your own by noticing when you're in the right place at the right time and grabbing opportunities with both hands. You've got to be in it to win it.

WORK HARDER THAN EVERYBODY ELSE

I speak to so many people who want to build their own brand, "find the magic", quickly without the willingness to put in the hard work. Before I started Tyrrell's, I worked in the fields for many years for 18 hours a day, went bankrupt and spent ten years building up another business before hitting upon my first big success. Once we started manufacturing the chips, I was on the factory floor every day and looking after all aspects of the business, from packaging and marketing to sales and distribution. We are all different but my theory is if I ask somebody to do a job then I would expect myself to be able to do it too.

TRUST IN YOURSELF, BUT LEARN FROM YOUR MISTAKES

When I first came up with my idea for Tyrrell's Chips, many people thought that I was daft. My trading business was going well, so why would I want to risk it all for something new? If I'd listened, I would never have done it and you wouldn't be reading this book. Instead, I'd still be at the end of one of my many phones selling spuds. Nobody has a divine right to be successful – just go for it.

TAKE INSPIRATION FROM OTHERS, BUT MAKE YOUR BRAND YOUR OWN

Tyrrell's was not the first premium chips brand in the UK, but our product was unique to us. I actually got the idea to use vintage black and white photographs on the packaging from a big supermarket's own brand and then went out and found images that fit our product and that's what became the talking point. Williams Chase came about because some rich Americans that I met at a Caribbean resort left behind a bottle of potato vodka at their table and it sparked an idea. Enter the UK's first field-to-bottle, single estate premium vodka and gin.

GET THINGS DONE

This is another simple to write, difficult to do sentence: a lot of people are talkers but not finishers. You must commit to doing something and then do it. Trust me, there are times when it's all going to seem too hard, when the easiest – and potentially safest option – is to walk away. But where would that get you? It's when situations get extreme that you're most likely to prosper and

it's much better, in my opinion, to regret some of the things you do rather than wonder 'what if?'.

MARKET YOUR BUSINESS

Forget all the fancy terms – marketing is just good communication. People will either like something or they don't, but it's you who has the power to capture their attention. Yes, the quality of the product and its packaging are important, but more often than not it's the story behind it that sells.

I've always been really careful when it comes to advertising. It's expensive and I'd rather spend the money to make sure that we are producing the very best spirit in the hope that people buy it on the back of its taste and how it's made. I've only ever done it sparingly, promoting our brands in speciality magazines, aiming to communicate with my customers as though they're friends. You can write your brand in the sky in neon lights, but nobody will notice it, to get the message across people have to discover you. With both Tyrrell's and Williams Chase, our *raison d'etre* has been the same: using our English potatoes to make a premium product on a single site.

Word-of-mouth has been the biggest influence on my businesses – I like people to discover our products, think that they're cool as well as delicious, and then share them with their friends. And if you're making something authentic, and you genuinely communicate this, then you're on the road to getting noticed.

NOBODY HAS THE ANSWERS

I may have been a terrible student, but I've spent my whole life being curious. I like to understand how things work and what makes people tick – and if you keep your eyes and your ears open you'll spot opportunities where others only see insurmountable brick walls. I also think you should always listen to advice – even if you don't agree with it as it's impossible to know it all and there are always things to learn.

CELEBRATE THE GOOD, DEAL WITH THE BAD

I'm one of those unfortunate people who lives life on an emotional rollercoaster. Most days I'm raring to go and wanting to set the world on fire. I take full advantage of my high days, pushing myself to the limit.

Along with the highs, I've come to expect the lows. It's on these rare occasions that I'm no good to anybody and it's better that I stay out of the way of anybody else and wait for the feelings to pass, which they inevitably do.

TRY TO STAY BALANCED

Building your own business is incredibly stressful. Not only do you need to look after yourself and your family, you've also got employees who rely on you to keep your business afloat.

When I was younger I could be volatile. I used to get very angry when people made a mistake or didn't commit to the business as much as I did.

My tempers have not been my finest moments. I've mellowed a lot since then and now with Williams Chase I'm very much hands off. Mistakes happen and you have to learn to give them the perspective they deserve and respond appropriately.

DON'T BE ARROGANT

Once you've reached a certain level of success it's easy to let yourself become too confident. You might think that you've got all the answers once you've started earning money, but arrogance is the perfect way to alienate people and your brand.

Success does breed success.

EVERYDAY IS A LIFETIME

An old farmer told me once that it's not until you're in the winner's enclosure that you realise the fun was in the race. Yes, working for yourself is hard. Yes, there'll be days when we all want to quit. But if you don't enjoy what you're doing for the most part, then what's the point? If you're only in it for the money, then you're likely to lose motivation.

A few years ago when I was looking to buy a gorgeous vineyard in the Rhone Valley, France, I asked the guy who was selling it why he was moving on. 'Because I don't sing in the shower in the mornings,' he replied. He was 65 at the time and had owned the vineyard for fifteen years. 'I'm bored,' he added. 'I want to go and study modern history now.' I think there's a lesson here for all of us. If you're not 'singing in the shower' over what you do and can't find the magic, go and find something else.

ACT WITH INTEGRITY

When you're tired and feel like you're getting nowhere fast, it's easy to succumb to cutting corners, but doing so will only make your life harder in the long run. Back in my potato trading days, I went on a business trip to Turkey to see if importing their fruit and vegetables was a viable way for me to expand my business. And though the margins were good with what they were offering me and I could've made a lot more money, I didn't like the fact that I had to compromise myself to be able to do business with them. I had a bad hunch and it was an area that I didn't understand. In the end, I walked away.

HAVE A GOOD STORY

Where's the magic? Is it in the branding? Packaging? Quality of the product? To some extent, yes, but you're really onto something if you've got a good story to back you up. This is what makes you unique to your customers. I've had the pleasure of being interviewed a number of times for both Tyrrell's and Williams Chase Distillery and the journalists always want to know about how I went bankrupt [page 15], how I took on Tesco [Page 42] and, most importantly, how all of my products have been produced on my own farm. The only thing is that it follows you all the time!

TRY TO HAVE NO REGRETS

Despite the arrogance and a number of poor business and personal decisions, I wouldn't be where I am if I hadn't gone through it all. When I went bankrupt I felt very sorry for myself and people thought I had a chip (no pun intended) on my shoulder. It wasn't fair. I'd worked really hard only to have all that effort seem like a complete waste of time. I learnt, however, to use it to my advantage and now I can say that it was a good thing. It also made me grow up and not take offence so easily. It was a valuable lesson, but a painful way to learn.

LEARN TO LET GO

My wife Kate believes that if something has passed its usefulness in our house, it gets chucked, recycled or given to charity immediately. I used to be more sentimental about saving things, but something changed when I sold Tyrrell's. The house that I grew up in, the one that I fought so hard to keep after I lost everything, also went in the sale.

KNOW YOURSELF

After selling Tyrrell's, I could've retired early and spent my remaining years retired. After working so hard for so many years, that kind of lifestyle didn't suit me. I needed another project and Williams Chase was just the ticket. Now I need another as writing this book has helped me see. It's only now that I've put it in black and white that I can actually see how far I've come and where I am at right now – though it's scary how much I've forgotten.

I am now a 50-something potato entrepreneur who spent his early life wanting to be older and his later life wanting the opposite. Off the back of the spud, I've created three good businesses and, with Williams GB Gin, a product that is the best thing I've made from potatoes to date.

DON'T BE BULLIED

There has been many occasions that people and companies both big and small have tried to control me. I could've let Tesco's cut my prices and allowed them to continue stocking my chips. I also could've let Chase Manhattan Bank bully me into changing the name of our vodka, but I didn't.

Most recently, we had issue with the branding for our Willy's Cider. The Portman Group – the body that overseas and regulates the industry – told us that we couldn't use the name because of its connotations with male genitalia. They also thought that I was marketing to underage drinkers. I wrote back and told them I was very offended by the insinuation, that Willy was nothing more than my nickname. I won this battle too. It's so easy to let yourself be pushed around, but you've got to show a bit of fight and stand up for what you believe in.

Team Chase: It takes a lot of people to grow, mash, ferment, distill, finish and hand bottle our spirits.

ONE SUCCESS DOESN'T GUARANTEE YOUR FUTURE

I made the mistake of thinking that I could do the same thing with spirits as I did with chips. I changed the way people ate chips, so why couldn't I change the way people drank vodka?

As it turns out, the same rules didn't entirely apply in the spirits industry so we had to change our strategy. In some ways, starting a premium vodka distillery in 2008 was probably the worst thing you could do. The economy was crashing and our product, because of how costly it is to make, is both premium and expensive.

Consumers, however, were also becoming more aware of where their food and drink came from, and because our spirits are made from field to bottle, we were able to capitalise on that. It's the concept of traceability, made more important as a result of the 2013 horsemeat, BSE and foot and mouth disease scandals, that convinced us to switch gears and turn our business around.

Vodka's reputation as a cheap spirit has also led us to regroup. Gin has pedigree in the UK, so we decided to move into that market as well. Our elegant gin is made with our cider spirit from our cider apples, while our GB gin is made from our potato vodka and distilled with juniper and our secret mix of special botanicals.

YOU CAN NEVER DO TOO MUCH FOR YOUR CUSTOMERS

Everyone remembers bad customer service. Nobody wants to be treated like just another number. When the phone rings, make sure it's a human that answers. Customers are the backbone of your business, no matter its size. A lot of businesses, particularly successful ones, get too full of themselves and forget that without their customers it would all be over. Treat everyone with respect. Don't be tight or mean. Try to understand their needs and go above and beyond to fulfil them – even if it means offering to stack their shelves for them.

KEEP THE BUSINESS GODS HAPPY

I have not met or seen the business gods, but I know they exist. To keep them on your side you must be honest, trustworthy and provide a genuine product or service. Don't cut corners. Don't be fake. The truth always comes out in the end.

George Shropshire and Caroline Clarke at Wimbledon, 2009

Rock the Farm

Our very own festival for bartenders, hosted at our farm distillery.

'Music, open fields, good food and drink... what more could you ask for? A distillery, and a whole lot of bartenders - that's what'

IMBIBE MAGAZINE, 2014

OUT OF THE FRYER

From gin to grenache

Author Peter Mayle and Kate Chase

Out of the fryer and into the fire

And here ends my story with potatoes.

I'm now passing the potato mantle on to my sons Harry and James and the team at Williams Chase, but that doesn't mean that I'm sailing off into the sunset. I can't ever imagine retiring – I always want a reason to get out of bed and the buzz of learning something new and that never-ending search for the magic.

Whisky has been on my mind since I went on a sales trip to Japan in 2009 and got a taste of what they've been up to. I've got my own attempts at the distillery, ageing in various barrels that I've sourced from all over the world. The first batch is 5-years old and I want to release it in 2020. We're making about 200 casks a year, so this is a very long project, but one that is a lot of fun.

I've also got plans for starting a cosmetics and skincare line with the left over botanicals from our distilling process. This is a difficult one as in the past most of these products have emerged from scientific labs and to do this I need someone who is really interested in it. Could that be you? Send me your CV.

My big love now, however, is wine and for the last couple of years I've been making my own at Chateau Constantin near the village of Lourmarin – a small southern French village in the Rhone Valley. I also have a negoce business sourcing other barrels of fine Burgundy and Rhone wines, but that's a whole other story which I'm planning to share in my next book. You see - I can't sit still...

I'd love to hear where the magic is for you,

William Chase, October 2015
Will@williamschase.co.uk
#willsstory

Acknowledgements

Writing this book over the last six months has been an amazing experience. Reflecting on the past 35 years of my life has released all the ups and downs during that time, from focusing on potatoes in my 20s to how that led to Tyrrell's and Williams Chase.

No man is an island, however, and the only way all this came together was with the support of all the wonderful people round me. There is no particular order to the following thanks yous and it's very difficult because there are so many people involved, but here I go.

Naturally, I would like to thank my late mother Sam and father Leonard, as without them none of this would have been possible. They say you don't really respect what your parents did for you until you have children of your own, and I know mine had to put up with me being a very difficult child. I also want to say a very big thank you to my stepmother, June Chase, for standing firmly by my side in my hour of need and for introducing me to her friend David Surridge. Not only did June, with David's assistance, help me secure the funds to raise Tyrrell's Court Ltd from the ashes, she personally guaranteed my loan, risking her own house in the process. Thank you so much, June. Without

you things would have been totally different.

To all the local farmers and landowners, including the late David Corbett, David and Brian Speakman, Philip Houlbroke, Tom and Pip Davies, John Cawley, Charlie Hanson, John Bill Thomas, Derek Thomas, Paul Young, the late Michael Weaver and many more. These great people stood by me, gave me credit, rented me their land and/or trusted their potatoes with me. There are so many other businesses that helped me too. Barclay's bank manager David Owen also deserves a special mention. Remembering the support you all gave me is making me quite emotional. Thank you all for making my potato and farming days possible and helping me get back on my feet. When you're on the floor it's tough to get up and you were all there for me.

Thank you to everyone who worked over and above to get Tyrrell's up and running and made it what it is today: Ian Parkinson, Andrew Jones, Karen Powell, Debbie Bliss, Val Keys, Rachel Davies, Janice Bennett, Mark Hammond, Julie Lewis, Tony Fenn and all the other fantastic people who gave 100 per cent of themselves to build something they believed in, especially in the early days. 'Put it to go' is a Herefordshire saying that means making something happen, and without these people Tyrrell's would never have got off the ground. I also want to mention all the independent retailers and suppliers who bought into my story so much that it felt as though we traded as friends.

I would like to thank our team at Williams Chase for helping me on such a fantastic spirits adventure by creating the World's best tasting vodka. I couldn't have done it without you. I would also like to thank all of the people involved in the creation of this book as everybody who knows me knows that I am not the easiest person to get on with and have a very short concentration span. Initially I looked at working with other publishing firms. Not only was it expensive, I was also worried that the end result wouldn't convey my true personality, so I decided to create Single Estate – our publishing house, enabling us to write and publish it ourselves.

A very special and big thank you goes to Kate McAuley for working with me over the last six months to get the content in place. A special thanks also goes to my son James Chase for the cocktails, Callum McDonald, our chef at Verzon House, for the recipes, Becca Wild for her beautiful food and drink photography, and Lorna Hollings for helping me dig out all the pictures from our archives. The team at Orphans Press in Leominster also

deserves a mention. The book has been completely made in Herefordshire and it's as close as I could make it to being the genuine article.

Finally, I'd like to thank my wife Kate Chase for putting up with my absences and my moods over the last six months. Pulling this book together was a fun, yet difficult process – trying not to upset anybody, unable to mention everybody and physically telling my story in a way that I hope you found interesting. I don't have all the answers and there is no book of rules. I just wanted to share these events with you and hope that you will find your magic too. I'd like to add a very big thanks to you too for picking up One Potato, Two... and taking the time to read my story.

It's now time for me to move onto the next chapter.

Kate McAuley

Editor

My first meeting with William Chase was the result of a happy accident. A friend had won a free weekend at Verzon House along with a tour of Chase Distillery and I was lucky enough to be invited along as her plus one.

As a food and travel writer by profession, I was intrigued by the spirits (especially the gin), but hadn't really given the trip a great deal of thought. Mostly, I was looking forward to a relaxing weekend in the country and perhaps going on a walk across the nearby Malvern Hills. All that changed when William stopped by for a chat. I was riveted from the get-go.

Although I love my work, I'd become a little jaded. The food and drink industry seemed to me to be full of a whole lot of gimmicks and razzle-dazzle. Companies who were trading as authentic, turned out to be nothing of the sort once you started to scratch the surface, while marketing teams rather than chefs and restaurateurs seemed to be setting food trends. Where was the substance?

William, needless to say, was a breath of fresh country air. His overarching passion for Herefordshire and insatiable curiosity coupled with his desire for making products with, provenance and pedigree, we're an intoxicating (no pun intended) mix.

'You should write a book,' I said. 'Funny you should say that,' he said. And the rest, as they say, is history. I was looking for another big project and I wanted to work on something that excited me, and William's story was perfect.

And thus began months of talking, planning and writing. This is a tale that has a bit of everything – bouncing back after failure, David-and-Goliath-style battles, the romance of the English countryside and how believing in yourself no matter what can lead to success. Needless to say it's been an absolute honour and privilege to work with William on this book and I'm so proud of the end result.

Kate McAuley
@its_katemcauley

Orphans
Design & Production

S omething is afoot in the sleepy county of Herefordshire. We've always been known for our agriculture and the rich quality of our produce, from apples and pears to beef and potatoes. But now the producers have turned marketers, with an entrepreneurial flair and confidence unknown when we were printing only simple potato box labels 30 years ago. We are now a county with many interesting brands and owners as aware of marketing as they are passionate about quality. Will Chase has been the pioneer of this new spirit and his vision and success have sewn a seed which has inspired many to follow in his footsteps. Its also given opportunity to service providers like ourselves and in turn we have re-shaped our business to become marketing and design focussed with website development as well as printing. The one constant in this renaissance for all things Herefordshire is the quality of the product. Its a bedrock Will continues to champion and sets the tone for our design and production. We've enjoyed playing our part in the book and we've loved the journey to here. Better still, we know there's more to come. A lot more!

DIAGEO

Edinburgh Park
5 Lochside Way
Edinburgh
EH12 9DT

www.diageo.com

with compliments

Hi Liam – thought this book might
be of interest – catch up soon.

Cheers
Michael /.

JOHNNIE WALKER • Crown Royal • BUCHANAN'S • WINDSOR • DonJulio • SMIRNOFF • KetelOne VODKA • CÎROC • Captain Morgan • BAILEYS • Tanqueray • GUINNESS

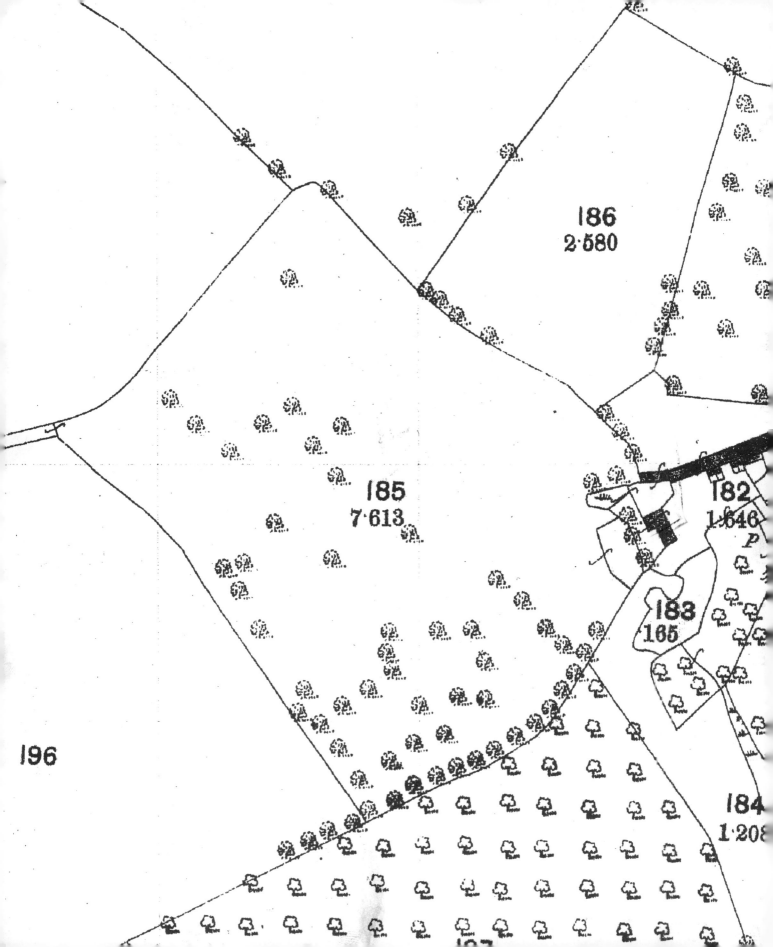

186
2·580

185
7·613

196

182
1·646

183
165

184
1·208